D0631400

BETWEEN RELIGIOUS ROCKS
AND LIFE'S HARD PLACES

Charles + Alma Green

BETWEEN RELIGIOUS ROCKS
AND LIFE'S HARD PLACES

*101 Answers to Tough Questions
about What You Believe*

GREG ALBRECHT

Published by
THOMAS NELSON
Since 1798

www.thomasnelson.com

Copyright © 2006 by Greg Albrecht

All rights reserved. No portion of this book may be reproduced, stored in a retrieval system, or transmitted in any form or by any means—electronic, mechanical, photocopy, recording, scanning, or other—except for brief quotations in critical reviews or articles, without the prior written permission of the publisher.

Published in Nashville, Tennessee, by Thomas Nelson, Inc.

Thomas Nelson, Inc. titles may be purchased in bulk for educational, business, fund-raising, or sales promotional use. For information, please e-mail SpecialMarkets@ThomasNelson.com.

Unless otherwise indicated, all Scripture passages are from the Holy Bible, New International Version® (NIV), copyright © 1973, 1978, 1984 by International Bible Society. Used by permission of Zondervan Publishing House. All rights reserved.

Library of Congress Cataloging-in-Publication Data

Albrecht, Greg, 1947-
  Between religious rocks and life's hard places : 101 answers to tough questions about what you believe / Greg Albrecht.
     p. cm.
  Includes bibliographical references and index.
  ISBN-13: 978-0-529-12228-5 (alk. paper)
  ISBN-10: 0-529-12228-6 (alk. paper)
  1. Theology, Doctrinal--Popular works. 2. Christianity--Miscellanea.
  I. Title.
  BT77.A295 2006
  230--dc22

2006024356

Printed in the United States of America
06 07 08 09 RRD 6 5 4 3 2 1

CONTENTS

ACKNOWLEDGMENTS

Writers look forward to being edited like they look forward to their next visit to the dentist for a root canal. I know, because I find myself on both ends of the "procedure."

Authors often compare writing a book with giving birth to a child—of course, only mothers who then become authors truly have the right to use this metaphor.

This is my third book published by the Nelson family of publishers, and each experience has been unique, not unlike the circumstances surrounding the pregnancy and birth of a child (or so I am told!). This book has been easier than the first two (am I sounding like a mother or what?)—perhaps because I've been through this process before and I now know what to expect. That may be part of the equation, but another important element has been the entire team at Thomas Nelson. My primary editor has been Ramona Richards, who made sure that each time I left the dentist's chair I did so feeling like there was hope for tomorrow!

My sincere thanks to everyone who helped produce this book.

This book would not have been possible without thousands of people I will probably never meet, at least on this side of eternity. Thousands of people in cyberspace have talked with me, sharing their joys and heartaches, asking me to be of whatever help I could with their questions about the Bible, religion, and faith. Thanks to each and every one of you for your questions.

My co-workers at Plain Truth Ministries have also contributed to the manuscript through proofreading and editing. My sincere thanks to Monte Wolverton, Laura Urista, and my wife Karen, all of whom played their part in the selection and editing of the questions and answers we share with you.

Most importantly, thanks be to God for His unending and matchless grace, which He first started to reveal to me almost twenty years ago. God's grace gave my life meaning, direction, and significance it never had before, and it is only because of His grace that I may, in some minor way, reflect the light of Jesus Christ.

INTRODUCTION

There *are* more questions than answers. The older I get, the more convinced I am that I will die with many unanswered questions. While there is truth in the cliché "you can't take it with you," I do anticipate taking a long list of questions to heaven.

There was a time, earlier in my life, when I believed being uncertain about any issue was a sign of spiritual weakness. At the time, my fundamentalist worldview insisted that I wasn't supposed to have questions; I was supposed to have answers—all of the answers. Religions that pretend to have all the answers don't encourage questions. I was a spiritual know-it-all, living in a fool's paradise assuming I had an answer for any and all questions. One day, by God's grace, I came to the startling revelation that there are questions for which there aren't cut-and-dried answers.

This is not to say I buy into the politically correct contemporary notion that the only absolute truth is that there are no absolutes, a philosophical maxim that has been enthroned as the bottom line of law and morality. I absolutely believe that there are absolutes. It's just that I believe there are far fewer absolutes than I once fervently believed.

One of the hallmarks of both emotional and spiritual health is the maturity of knowing that life is filled with ambiguity—

and that we cannot put all of life's dilemmas into neat and tidy categories. Knowing that there are gray areas of life and realizing that we humans are incapable of perfect and precise judgments is a sign of a healthy and well-balanced spiritual life.

About ten years ago, I decided to invite online questions about faith, religion, and the Bible as a part of my ministry (see www.ptm.org). I was convinced then that a need existed, and today, a decade of questions later, I am even more convicted of that need. People who send a question are able to do so anonymously, for I do not ask them to provide any personal information. It's a superb atmosphere for asking questions, because those asking questions know I don't know their identity, where they live, how old they are, or what they know or do not know about the subject of concern. This freedom has allowed safe self-disclosure for tens of thousands who have directed queries my way, inquiries they may not otherwise have asked.

I tackle this adventure much like a radio talk show—my answers are as spontaneous as possible. Of course, a call-in radio show usually has a screener, who helps the host determine whether the caller will be given airtime. While I do the screening myself, and thus I see all the questions, I am like a radio talk show host in cyberspace in that time does not permit me to send a personal answer for each request.

It's been an incredible journey for me—tens of thousands of questions into this adventure, I am more firmly convinced that the world of religion remains muddled, mystifying, and mysterious to many, if not most.

One of my tasks in this venture is to equip people with the necessary tools and methodology to face issues and come to their own independent, Christ-centered conclusions. I believe that Christianity is first of all based on faith—faith that God exists and that He is who He says He is. But Christian faith is not blind. Biblical revelation of God is logical and coherent. We are created in God's image, which, among other things, means that He has designed us to think, ponder, imagine, and bring cognitively critical faculties to bear as we face dilemmas.

The God of the Bible cannot only be known, but the chief end in life is to know the only true God and Jesus Christ whom He has sent (John 17:3). Jesus came to reveal the Father, and the gospel of Jesus Christ is based on God's amazing grace. Thus, answers to issues that challenge us should be based on God's grace and centered in the person and work of Jesus Christ.

My experience in fielding questions over the past decade has given me a greater appreciation of the fact that we humans are all too willing to yield our freedom to religious experts and have them tell us what and how to think. But as Christians, we are all priests and believers (1 Peter 2:9), called to prepare our minds for action (1 Peter 1:13) so that we can individually give our own answers (1 Peter 3:15) that are grounded in our faith. My goal is to help direct those whom I serve to God so that they believe in Him rather than some glib answer I may provide.

There are times when some seem to regard me somewhat like an online religious recipe consultant. As they pour their question into the keyboard of their computer, they are often in the middle of some kind of religious crisis of faith or some confusing religious experience. They are busy in their religious kitchen, trying to determine how to make the religious recipes of their lives turn out. Thus, their questions often are all about how much of a particular ingredient should be used and how long must the recipe be cooked, whipped, beaten, baked, or boiled. How many, how much, how often?

I believe that such foundational presuppositions must

themselves be challenged, for it is often the world of religion at large that has confronted us with religious concoctions and contrivances that frustrate us. There are times when the questioner wants no more than a simple way out; they wish for me to write them a prescription, describe a potion, or recommend an elixir that can get them out of their predicament.

Several years ago, during discussions with my publisher, this book started to take form. Over time, we all came to see that selected questions and answers, in book form, might be a valuable resource. I have selected some of the most representative questions and answers about the Bible, faith, and religion of the past decade, asked many times in a variety of ways. All of the questions in this book are edited versions of actual questions, originally asked in some form over the Internet. If you have visited www.ptm.org, you might even recognize one of your own questions in the following pages!

It is true that there are no stupid questions, only stupid answers. Assuming this cliché proves true somewhere in this collection of answers, remember as well that there is often more than one answer for any given question! If you don't like mine, improvise your own Christ-centered solution! It is my prayer that this collection will answer some questions for you, but more than that, I pray that you will discover and ponder even more questions in the process. May God bless you, may He continue to fill your mind with questions, and either because of or in spite of the answers I provide, may He even give you a few answers!

BETWEEN RELIGIOUS ROCKS
AND LIFE'S HARD PLACES

CHRISTIANITY

Is Christianity a religion?

Q *I've heard you use the word* religion *in a negative way. How do you define* religion? *What is the difference between Christian and Christian religion? Some application forms ask, "What is your religion?" What's a good answer?*

A I make a critical distinction in the definition of the word *religion.* I define *religion* as any belief system or methodology that promises God's love and blessings in return for human effort and performance. This definition is a sub-definition of the commonly used definitions for *religion,* i.e., 1) serving and worshipping God; 2) commitment to or devotion to faith, as in attending church *religiously*; 3) institutionalized attitudes, beliefs, and regulations.

Under the generally accepted definitions in our society and culture, Christianity is a religion. However, when it comes to biblical Christianity, and the precise examples and teachings we are given in the New Testament, religion cannot apply to Christ-centered and grace-based faith. In fact, religion then becomes the very opposite of authentic Christianity.

The main difference between Christianity and religion is that all religion is based on human performance. Religion teaches that human deeds and compliance are necessary for humans to earn God's favor. Authentic Christianity teaches that God's favor is given to us on the basis of His goodness, not because of human goodness.

If a person asks about your religious preference for the purpose of demographics/reports/surveys, then they are not looking for, nor would they necessarily understand, the critically important nuance we are discussing. In such a case, I answer "Protestant"—for I am a Christian, and a Protestant Christian, as compared to the two other major divisions of Christianity: Eastern/Russian/Greek Orthodox or Roman Catholic.

In my case, "Protestant Christian" isn't a complete definition. I'm an irreligious Protestant Christian. I reject religion but embrace and believe in Jesus Christ. That distinction is important. In particular, I reject the rigidity of religious fundamentalism. My rejection of religion, as performance on our part which predisposes God to favor us, is based on the biblical teaching of God's amazing grace. Everything that's popularly believed to be a stereotype of Christianity and every organized church within Christendom is not necessarily an accurate reflection of the teachings of Jesus Christ.

Those mean, nasty, hateful Christians . . .

Q *It seems that our society is becoming tolerant of most everything except Christianity. Why is this? Could it be that the love Christians are to show is offset by fire-and-brimstone preaching condemning to hell those who do not comply?*

A Has Christianity been so marred by inaccurate representations of God that many have determined that

2

Christians at large are bigots, fear-mongers, hateful, and nasty people? I heard of one survey that determined that the least desired potential next-door neighbor in the United States is a fundamentalist Christian. Some might say that's because many people don't want Christians next door making them feel guilty. Perhaps. But it's also true that most people can get by without a relentless diet of criticism and condemnation.

Has Christendom missed the primary emphasis of the gospel of Jesus Christ? Is the gospel really more about hell than it is about heaven? Is it more about doing stuff and following rules, regulations, and rituals—or is it more about God's love, mercy, and grace? If Jesus showed up today in our towns and cities, in our schools and courtrooms, in our cafes and malls, and yes, in our churches—would we recognize Him? Would He resemble what our churches have taught us? Would religion welcome Him? How closely would He echo the outspoken and reactive Christianity that is accepted as the norm by many?

Are Catholics Christians?

Q Is there a difference between a Christian and a Catholic?

A No, there isn't necessarily any difference between a Christian and a Catholic, or a Christian and a Lutheran, or a Christian and a Baptist. On the other hand, not all Catholics, Lutherans, or Baptists are Christians simply because of their membership in a specific denomination. Christianity is a personal relationship between God and humans, and no human organization has the exclusive right to represent God on earth.

Some doubt that there are any Christians at all in certain

churches, and some Protestants typically have this view toward Catholics. This issue goes back to the Reformation, to Martin Luther, almost five hundred years ago.

For Protestants to write off all Catholics as non-Christians because the church to which they belong officially supports Maryology, prayers to saints, and other unbiblical practices is to dismiss the sovereignty and power of God. God has His people everywhere—and no one person, no one church, can encompass or identify all Christians. We can thank God for that, for if someone or some church could identify all Christians, and everyone else who was not a Christian (in fact, there are some sects and cults that make this claim), this insight would lead to a host of problems.

How sad that many Protestants doubt whether Catholics are Christians. Equally so, many Catholics doubt whether Protestants are Christians. Jesus said that Christians would be known by their love. Instead, it seems we're often known as rock throwers!

When your adult children test your Christianity

Q   *Our unmarried, twenty-year-old son and his girlfriend just recently had a little baby girl. I seem to have a problem accepting this little baby as my grandchild. I'm a Christian, but I'm having a tough time dealing with all of this. I love our son, but I don't agree with what he has done.*

A   Sometimes we are worried that our love and acceptance will be misunderstood, so we do not express the love we feel. We can often be more concerned with the need to "take a stand" than we are with loving our family and friends. Sometimes, in our zeal to hate/condemn/denounce/take a stand against sin, love and acceptance often get lost.

Grace tells us that God loves us unconditionally. We are not used to this kind of love, and we are often confused when confronted with it. We find it difficult to either accept or express unconditional love. It sounds "too good to be true." Our culture is an "I will scratch your back if you scratch mine" society. We even barter our acceptance in relationships. Parents say—or at least communicate nonverbally—"I will love you if you get good grades," "I will love you if you do what I think you ought to," etc. But that kind of love is easy. It's simply saying, "You make me look good, feel good, appear successful, and I will love you in return."

That is not what God's love for us is based on—thank God! Because we are sinful, and it is impossible to bring home a perfect report card to God, we cannot do what we need to do without His love. We cannot earn His love and respect. He tells us that His grace is sufficient, that He loves us in spite of our sin and failure. He loves us unconditionally. This does not mean God wants us to sin, and that no matter how malicious we might be He will forget about it. Such an idea makes a mockery of grace.

God loved us enough to become one of us. In Jesus, God came to us, adding flesh to His divinity in order to save us from our sin. The process of becoming human was an enormous act of humility and love on God's part. He chose to be born to a young, unmarried girl, choosing to become a baby who was regarded as illegitimate by other humans He had Himself created. It was not easy to grow up in a small town in the land we know today as Israel with questionable parentage. There is no doubt that people did the math—they compared the date of Joseph and Mary's marriage with Jesus' age and talked about the fact that Jesus was older than He ought to have been, gossiping about how His parents must not have waited until they were married. Jesus has personal experience with the situation facing you and your family. He's lived through it, in the flesh.

Jesus has borne all of our sins and all of our sorrows. He is there for you now—today, and tomorrow, as you work with this relationship—a) a little baby granddaughter, b) your son, and, if he eventually marries his girlfriend, c) your daughter-in-law. This will not be easy to work through, but in Jesus you have someone who knows all about this. Talk to Him about it, and ask Him to fill you with His love.

You may want to ask God to help you love this precious little granddaughter without reservation or condition. After all, your granddaughter had nothing to do with the circumstances surrounding her conception and birth. As a grandparent, you are able to provide an important relationship that children don't have with their parents, and, in turn, grandchildren can add a dimension to your life that you would otherwise not enjoy.

Is becoming a better person the goal of Christianity?

Q *I am confused. Someone told me that the main thing Christians should do is to become better people and in turn make the world a better place. I want to be a better person and I want to help change the world, but isn't Christianity more than that?*

A Exactly! Christianity is more than a checklist of rules that help to make us and others better. The gospel of Jesus Christ is not primarily about morality. The gospel of Jesus

Christ is not a self-help program. The gospel of Jesus Christ is not a formula. It is not a careful regimen of popping religious pills to make us better, nor does it consist of religious programs that will give us more purpose, or following religious prescriptions that will help us avoid sin. Christianity is not one and the same as being moral.

Some of the most moral people alive today are not Christians. Moral people may or may not be Christians. Christians are moral, no doubt about that, but morality is not the goal and it is not the answer. The answer and the goal is Jesus. That's it. Jesus. Jesus produces morality in Christians, but morality alone does not produce Jesus. Building character may change what we do, but it does not change who we are. Jesus alone can change us from the inside out. He alone makes us into new men and women, because as our risen Lord He lives His resurrected life in us.

If morality alone is the goal of Christianity, then Jesus is completely unnecessary. If we can fix our own problems, then who needs Jesus? If we believe that we can produce enough goodness to turn our world around, then knowing Jesus, accepting Him, believing and trusting in Him, are irrelevant. The problem with proposing morality as the primary religious answer and goal is that Jesus is reduced to an afterthought, a religious ornament, a nice piece of religious furniture that we look at and admire but that has no practical value.

The gospel is not a program or club that we join so that we can help change the world. The gospel of Jesus Christ is not a matter of us looking at how wrong other people are and devising programs so that those people can qualify to become like us. Religious, special, better-than-everybody-else societies are not the answer. Religious formulas, programs, and initiatives are not the answer. Jesus alone is the answer.

FORGIVENESS

Will God forgive my adultery?

Q *I grew up in a Christian family. When I was married to my first husband, we were both Christians who then strayed away from God, and I eventually committed adultery. When my husband found out, I left him. He attempted suicide, but after he recovered, he said he forgave me and wanted me back. Then he began to beat me, so I left again. He divorced me. I remarried, and after a few years we both cheated on each other. Now, years later, I have found my way back to church. I have repented, but I can't find any peace. Is it possible that God won't forgive me for committing adultery? I really want to serve God, but I just have so many questions and no answers.*

A Your question—your guilt and worry—is a great example of why the gospel of Jesus Christ is such incredibly good news. No matter what we have done, no matter how many low places we have occupied, God loves us and will take us back, without recrimination. As you note, those who accept Christ may fall into sins and behaviors that are the very opposite of Christian virtues and practices, and the sad fact is such a thing happens in the lives of many.

When we ask God to forgive us, it is not possible for Him to say, "I don't forgive you," for that is not the way God is. You may not have forgiven yourself, and perhaps others may not forgive you. However, if you seek forgiveness from God, He will (and has, if you already have asked Him for forgiveness) forgive you. God does not forgive us if we don't wish to be forgiven. He doesn't forgive us against our will. He doesn't forgive us unless and until we seek His forgiveness. But when we do, His forgiveness is given, no questions asked—no stipulations and no conditions.

Forgiving racism

Q I am having a problem with forgiveness. I am a member of a racial minority. Before my husband (of another race) and I were married, my father-in-law shared his racist views openly. I was caught off guard the first time he shared his views. I looked to my soon-to-be husband to "clear up" the situation, but he did not support me. Years have passed, but I am unable to forgive my father-in-law or my husband for not standing up for me. This family claims to be Christian, but of a different denomination than I am. I find myself frustrated and filled with anger as if the events happened yesterday. My question is, as a Christian, what is my obligation to respect my elders and hold my tongue when I find my father-in-law's speech offensive? Do I hold my tongue for the sake of the relationship?

A There is no need for you to suffer in silence, without telling your father-in-law and your husband about the hurt they have caused—and may continue to cause. There are several issues here, with racism apparently being a major part of your pain. Racism, of course, includes the thesis that those who are not part of our specific racial family are inferior to us.

There are times when many have felt that it's better to "leave well enough alone" in these kinds of painful circumstances that you describe, fearing that if you rock the boat, things will get worse. In such cases, many continue to suffer in silence, and beyond that, anger, hatred, and animosity build and build internally until finally exploding in resentment. Nothing in the Bible suggests that we must allow ourselves to be a doormat for such treatment.

Sometimes, when something like this has been left unaddressed for so long, it has festered and become so painful that when we do bring it up it is hard for us to do so without lashing out in a vindictive way. It is hard to humbly, calmly, and lovingly let a loved one know that what they have done and, more importantly, what they continue to say and do, is hurting us. At such a time, it may be helpful for us to tell the other party that we know we should have said something earlier. On the other hand, the fact that we said nothing does not justify or excuse the painful things they said or did.

You mention the topic of respecting our elders. Yes, we should, but Paul told us all as children to "obey your parents in the Lord" (Ephesians 6:1). We are not under any obligation as Christians to stand by when elders say or do painful things that are inappropriate by any definition. We need not subject ourselves to such actions when there is another alternative.

Forgiveness for what has been said and done is the next step, but it is a step that is best formally undertaken once we have done our best to clear the air and to stop "suffering in silence."

Must we divulge all our sins to our spouse?

 If a person who is married was once involved in activity that was not appropriate and did something very horrible,

then realized it was wrong and honestly repented to God, does that person need to tell his or her spouse? Will God still forgive that person if his or her repentance was sincere and they changed their behavior and got back in right standing with God?

A The situation you describe can be a complicated mixture between human and divine forgiveness, communication, responsibility, and relationship.

God does not forgive us based upon actions we take to remedy or fix situations. God forgives us based upon our acceptance of Christ as our Savior, based upon our request of His mercy and grace. Forgiveness is not based upon what we do; it is based upon what Christ has already done.

However, you describe a marital relationship and the dilemma of whether to tell a spouse about something that, at one point in time at least, they do not know. Such a situation is complex, and there is no easy answer. Some may say that honesty is always the best policy, but honesty does not necessarily involve telling everyone, including your spouse, about all of one's sins (or at least those sins we can remember). Some believe that if there is a chance of a spouse finding out about a sin, then the other spouse should confess and be the one to bring such a situation to their husband's or wife's attention. There is no easy solution, nor is there a one-size-fits-all answer to give about such a situation. The reason there is no one perfect answer to your question is based on:

1. We humans are imperfect.
2. We humans differ in many ways.

God, on the other hand, is:

1. Perfect
2. The same yesterday, today, and forever.

11

God does not forgive us based upon our good behavior, then throw our past in our face if we fall at some time in the future. We will never be able to perfectly please either God or another human based upon our impeccable moral behavior. God does for us what we cannot do for ourselves—that is at the heart of the gospel.

Put another way, we know that our eternal forgiveness and our eternal relationship with God are secure, safe, protected, and sure. As for those human relationships (and we are all part of them and contribute to them, of course)—that's another thing!

Tolerating sin

Q   *I find myself in a dilemma when it comes to tolerating behavior from "Christians" who turn their backs on Christ. I am not talking about people who have never heard the gospel. I am talking about people who have heard and at one point accepted it. My mother-in-law is purchasing a home with her boyfriend—she is in her sixties, and he is in his thirties! She has asked her son (my husband) to help them move to the new residence. We have talked with her about her choices and the consequences when she decided to move in with her boyfriend six months ago. She attends church regularly. Now they are buying this house together. I believe by helping her move, we are providing the acceptance and tolerance she needs to continue in her sin. My husband totally disagrees. He says he loves his mom, and while he doesn't agree with what she is doing, she has asked him for help and he is going to help her.*

I agree with "hate the sin and love the sinner." I love my mother-in-law enough to confront her. Tolerance is not love. Just as God disciplines us because He loves us, we also must hold each other accountable. What are your thoughts?

A Some points to ponder:
1. While you may disagree with your mother-in-law's claim to be a Christian, she is your mother-in-law. While you do not want to appear to condone certain activities, what will you accomplish by taking a stand? Doesn't your mother-in-law already know how you and your husband feel? How much more of a "stand" do you both need to take?

2. God does not withdraw His love from us when we do things that are wrong and sinful. He does not compromise His holiness and perfection, but there is never a time when we cannot access Him. A complete end of contact on your part may mean you or your husband would be unable to positively influence your mother-in-law.

3. You say that your mother-in-law attends church. But attendance at church does not mean that someone is a Christian. There are many people who have attended church all their lives but are not Christian. How do you know that your mother-in-law is truly a Christian? Perhaps the behavior you describe is one way of telling that she is not and never has been. You won't know unless you've talked extensively about this with her. She may need your friendship and contact now more than ever before.

4. You are correct, tolerance is not necessarily love. But it is also true that there are many times when we repel people when we think all we are doing is taking a stand. Above all, we want to be a tool, a vehicle that God can use to shine the light of Christ into other people's lives. And no, we do not want to compromise. But we want to be available, approachable, and open—therein lies the tension in this situation and the balance you seek.

How can I show love and compassion without condoning specific behavior?

Q *My cousin had a child out of wedlock. Some time after the birth, my family had a baby shower for her. My father, who is a Christian, did not feel it was right for him to attend due to the fact that the baby was born out of wedlock, and he believed his attendance would only show that he tolerated this behavior.*

However, at the same time, my father attended a funeral for a close friend of the family who committed suicide. I feel that he should have given the same support to my cousin. I hate to compare and contrast sins, but isn't it rather hypocritical of him?

A Your question seems to be this: if we attend an event with or have any kind of social contact with someone, does our presence communicate our agreement with their lifestyle and all of their specific behaviors? When Jesus initiated a conversation with a sinful woman by the well (John 4), did He intend that His conversation with her be taken as His approval of her past (she had lived with many men) or her present lifestyle (she was at the time living with another man)? By attending dinners in the homes of self-righteous religious people, was Jesus supporting them? Jesus' actions in allowing people to "touch" Him, such as lepers and the woman who let down her hair and washed His feet with it, scandalized "good" people.

We will not change people. We will not change their minds by boycotting a social occasion, particularly the events you describe. In such cases, surely we should ask ourselves why our actions are at odds with what it would seem Jesus would do, according to the Bible.

We cannot let the light of Jesus shine through us if we hide it, or in the words of Jesus, if we light our lamp and put it under a container of some kind (Matthew 5:15). We certainly can't help direct them to the glorious light of Christ if all they feel we do is condemn them.

BURIAL OR CREMATION

Does the Bible condemn cremation?

Q *Please explain cremation from a biblical, Christian view point. Is there anything wrong with being cremated?*

A Burial became the Christian practice following its Old Testament roots. Of course, Jesus was buried, but in a tomb, above ground, and in a very different way than our Western custom of burial in a casket. The Bible gives no specific burial practice, customs, or traditions that we must follow. For many years, Christian sailors have been buried at sea, for example. God does not need for us to be buried in a particular way so that He might resurrect us. Some bodies are so destroyed in accidents or in warfare that burial of the complete body is impossible.

Cremation is opposed by some Christians on the grounds that some "pagans" burn the bodies of their dead. That is true, but people who are not Christians also eat, breathe, marry, have children, etc. There is nothing in the Bible to suggest that cremation is an inferior practice to burial. A case might actually be made *for* cremation, as it is a much more responsible practice in areas where land is at a premium. In addition, some simply cannot afford a burial and cremation is the only economically viable option. There is nothing in the Bible that would condemn cremation.

CHURCH

When big churches become big business

Q *I live in Alabama, in the "Bible Belt." In our large cities, you find a gargantuan, red-brick church with huge white pillars almost every square mile. These churches have thousands of members, require tithing, and have large staffs, expensive furniture, multimillion-dollar budgets, and multimillion-dollar debt. Am I just being cynical, or am I right to question whether this is big business or whether it is Christianity?*

All they seem to talk about is money, growth, and expansion. It seems more like big business rather than the Great Commission. Don't get me wrong, I'm not saying that ministers shouldn't be compensated, but many pastors of these big churches live in huge houses, drive luxury cars, and wear expensive clothing and jewelry. I saw one pastor on TV asking for more donations for the church to buy a jet so that he could fly all over the world.

One church I visited gave me a membership handout that had six pages on the importance of tithing. Shouldn't we as Christians give according to how we have been blessed and not by Old Testament standards? Some of these churches are extremely exclusive—as if they see themselves as the only place in town to worship God properly. Aren't all believers members of Christ's church?

17

A I find your perspective to be informed, accurate, and, most importantly, Christ-centered. You are asking appropriate and important questions. In his book, *The Subversion of Christianity*, Jacques Ellul proposes that authentic Christianity functioned best when it was small, and that its very success in its early history became a source of corruption and perversion. The church was active, dynamic, and alive in Christ when small, but then when it grew large, a need arose for "storehouses" for its treasures. Bishops and bureaucracy soon reigned over treasuries and museums of fine art, all under the auspices of the work of the church!

Of course, the Bible makes clear that monetary success itself, inside or outside of the church, is not wrong. The love of money is not "the" root of all evil; it is "a" root. Not all mega-churches are monuments built to memorialize themselves, their founders, and their denominations. But there are big churches that do just that and more. The job of the church is to proclaim the gospel, to reach out, and to introduce Jesus to those who are in need (and remember that Jesus said those who know they have needs are easier to minister to than those who feel self-satisfied).

Your comments about mandatory, regulated, and enforced 10 percent tithing are right on the money (pun intended). The New Testament does not give churches permission to hammer people with any part of the Old Covenant, as if obedience to the Old Covenant is required for salvation. Christians are called to give, and give generously—and it's the job of the church to remind them of that. But a church oversteps its bounds if it insists on 10 percent. And, of course, many churches further overstep their bounds by implying that their church, congregation, or denomination has more truth, better truth, or a faster track to heaven than other churches. Such "truth claims" usually start as sincere attempts to motivate church members but can quickly become control devices to keep people in the pews of one church rather than drifting away to another.

One of the signs of a healthy church is its willingness not only to allow but to accept, with a generous spirit, those former members who determine, for a variety of reasons, to change their spiritual address to another healthy, well-balanced, Christ-centered church. If a healthy church expresses concern about a person leaving the church, then it should only be expressed when a person is moving to a cultic or toxic church. A healthy church is well within its God-given responsibility to proclaim the faith "once for all delivered to the saints" (Jude 3, ESV).

You are correct about the universal body of Christ—and again, belief in and acceptance of the universal church is a sign of authentic Christianity. Authentic Christians welcome the fact that the body of Christ is bigger than their own little church or denomination.

Is church really necessary?

Q *I was a member of a church for many years, which I now realize was a legalistic cult. As I have searched for another church to attend, I have come to wonder if we even need to belong to a church here on earth. To me, Jesus Christ is the One and Only True Church. We should all join His church and have a relationship with Him. I would like your input on this.*

A You raise several questions and issues—I'll try to offer some helpful comments:

1. Changing a church can be extremely painful and difficult. In some ways, it's like a divorce and second marriage. When

someone has been involved in one church for many years, they grow accustomed to a culture, worship traditions, and in-house terminology and language. In many situations, the new church never measures up because, in the mind of the individual, the first or original church (even if it was an unhealthy, toxic church) is always the standard by which other churches are judged.

2. Then there are those who change churches where the opposite dynamic is true. The original church was so bad and so ineffective, in their estimation, that any new church is virtually perfect and can do no wrong. They do not grieve their past church but have an attitude of "good riddance." The old church may have been a legalistic cult (as it seems to have been in your case), but that does not mean *all* other churches are spiritually healthy.

3. Those who believe that they have been burned out with church and/or religion constitute another perspective/dilemma. Many who feel "burned out" with church had a previous relationship with a church that promised them exclusivity—benefits and a relationship with God that no other church could match (at least according to the claim of the church). When the individual discovers major flaws and imperfections, they are often disillusioned. If they thought they were a part of the "one and only true church" only to find that their so-called "true" church had many flaws and failings, and that there are many Christ-centered churches, loss of faith can result.

As Christians, our primary spiritual relationship is with God—not a humanly incorporated entity that mediates between God and us. That does not mean that church attendance and involvement is not helpful; it can be. But faithful attendance at a church does not transform us into Christians any more than sitting in a barn makes us a cow or a horse. There are "good" churches and "bad" churches—healthy and unhealthy congregations (see also "Breaking free from legalism," page 162).

Searching for a church

Q *I am currently searching for a church. I have visited many. Which of all the churches is correct? I am confused. I love the Lord with all my heart, soul, and mind, and I have prayed about this. Help!*

A Perhaps we should begin with one of your last statements: "Which of all the churches is correct?" Here are some issues that should be considered when looking for a church home:

Christ-centered. A healthy church should be centered in Christ—His coming, His sacrifice on the cross, and His victorious resurrection.

Gospel-focused. A healthy church is focused on the gospel, not on glitz, excitement, or entertainment. A healthy church can be fun and interesting, but a church is not healthy simply because it is fun and interesting and makes us feel good.

Core teachings. A healthy church understands, upholds, and teaches the basic and core teachings of the historic Christian faith.

Recognizes all believers. A healthy church does not claim to have superior understanding, more knowledge, and better doctrines—and certainly does not tout itself as the only true church. One of the foundational and core beliefs of the historic Christian church is that the body of Christ is worldwide—that it is united—and that no one denomination encompasses the body of Christ.

21

Bible-centered. Preaching in a healthy church is centered in and on the Bible—not co-equally with the teachings and writings of the founding pastor or any other human leader.

Salvation by grace. A healthy church will understand and strongly warn of the dangers of legalism—teaching and believing that salvation is by faith alone, by Christ alone, by grace alone.

If you decide to become a member of a church, such a decision is not necessarily a life-long commitment. On the other hand, your spiritual relationship with God and with our Lord and Savior is an eternal commitment. Churches, congregations, and human beings come and go, but Jesus Christ is the same yesterday, today, and forever. Place your confidence and trust in Him.

"Buy the truth and sell it not"

Q *Proverbs 23:23 says, "Buy the truth and do not sell it." How can churches or ministries ask for money and sell books and ask for donations for things like seminars?*

A What does this verse in Proverbs actually mean? If it literally means that the truth can and should be purchased but that it cannot be sold, then we must logically assume that the only source from which we can buy the truth is from sinners who reject the truth—for if they accepted the truth, then they would not be selling it. So what source do we look for to purchase truth if this verse is to be taken as literally as you suggest?

The verse is a proverb, of course, explaining a principle in figurative language. It means that we should value truth, hold on to it, "invest" in it, "purchase" it, never let it go, and never sell it. You quote only part of the verse, which also says to "get wisdom, discipline and understanding."

The context of this passage is also helpful. Begin with verse 17, which speaks about a son who is admonished not to envy sinners, not to join those who drink too much or gorge themselves (v. 20)—for drunkards and gluttons (the self-indulgent) become poor. The son is told to listen to his father and mother and to *buy* (to be energetic in searching and working for and expending necessary resources) the truth and not to sell it.

If we took part of one sentence of this verse out of context, as you suggest, we might end up concluding that: 1) the very sources that one would go to for good sense, education, and truth would not be allowed remuneration for their services, and thus the sources would not be available; 2) that many other passages in the Bible, both Old and New Testaments, which speak of teachers and those who pastor being worthy of their hire, would all be nullified by an overly literal, out-of-context reading of one verse in the book of Proverbs. This is at best an unacceptable way to understand any of the Bible—and at worst a twisting and distorting of the Word of God.

Parables of Christ speak of a treasure in a field—a field that was purchased by a wise man because it contained treasure. He does not, nor does this proverb, forbid one from effort, sacrifice, and even financial expense to obtain something of value—in this case, truth.

This passage does not propose that teachers, pastors, professors, and authors of biblical truth should not be allowed to earn a living from their efforts to proclaim the gospel of Jesus Christ.

What does it mean to worship God?

Q *I see worship as showing your love for God. We might do this through singing, praying, or clapping hands. How* *would you describe worship, and where in the Bible may I find information on how to worship?*

A Worship is a big topic—one that has become, in terms of the definition given to the word, much more popular in Christian circles in the past few decades. Worship is the acceptance of who we are in relation to God—that He is God and we are not. Worship is the humility that God gives us to see ourselves as exactly who we are—in need of and dependent upon God rather than independent and without any need of Him.

Worship is also behavior and action in which humans voluntarily engage that is intended to acknowledge our position of need, while at the same time praising God for His unbelievable, unconditional love of us, the unlovable. He loves us not because we deserve His love; He loves us even though we are most undeserving. And the only reason we can even begin to fathom all of this is not because of our spiritual prowess or acuity, but because God gives us the ability to come to know Him. He gives us a relationship with Him by His grace. Nothing of spiritual value or consequence is because of us. Everything is because of Him. Consequently, when we call to mind all that God is, and who we are, there is no other human response but to worship.

Worship is not confined to any specific cultural response. Worship does not depend on a specific external act in which our bodies are involved or the posture we assume. Singing, prayer, joy, meditation, clapping, and dancing are only outward ways that we express what God is doing in our hearts. Any outward display we might define as worship can be divisive if we believe others must conform to a particular action, style, mode of music, expression, or gesture. Worship can then become legalism and idolatry, and it becomes a vain exercise that is all about us—not about God.

Help! My daughter is becoming a fundamentalist!

Q *I am a Christian and attend a community church. I raised my two daughters in the church as well. They were baptized at ten and twelve years old. They had both prayed to ask Jesus into their hearts and fully understood what becoming a Christian meant. My oldest daughter, now age eighteen, wants to marry a twenty-four-year-old neighbor boy who is a fundamentalist. She dove headfirst into his belief system. Now it's long skirts and hair pulled back!*

I would like some biblical ammunition to help her understand the freedom that we have through Christ. Until they break up, there will be no changing her mind, but I am afraid that they will be doing the customary "marry 'em young" thing. Plus, she has started the "Mom, you really should come to hear Brother so-and-so speak tonight" or "You really need to come to revival with me."

I don't want to push her farther into this life by rejecting her invitations, but I am a little bitter toward the fact that this relationship continued after I told the young man I did not approve. Anyway, I have experienced fundamentalism—my mother's dad was a preacher—and I have seen the life. I hope that you can give some insight into this. Mainly, how do I let her know that dressing according to certain man-made restrictions doesn't make her any better than she was a year ago or less "attractive to men"?

A Here are some general thoughts for you to consider:
1. What you describe is not a question about whether your daughter and her boyfriend are Christian—but a

relationship which involves some major denominational and cultural boundaries. Your daughter and the young man she is dating should give serious consideration to this issue.

In such situations, it's usually best to avoid becoming involved in discussing whether one faith tradition is right or wrong biblically, or whether one is better and superior to the other. Once that starts, little constructive communication will occur, but name-calling will soon be the inevitable result. But, at the same time, there are differences, and such differences may not seem important now to these two young people. However, they may well become important as time goes by, as children arrive, as decisions about which church to attend, which Christian culture to embrace, etc., have to be made. Responsible adults can help them face and discuss such issues.

2. Your daughter's age is very much an issue. The vast majority of all marriage counselors (Christian and non-Christian), as well as pastors in most Christian denominations, agree that eighteen is way too young. The individual has not yet decided who they are and what they want to do with their life.

Your daughter could benefit from counseling and advice on this topic, perhaps from some third-party, objective source who does not know either family, your daughter, or the young man. There may be another church in town, for example, that is not a part of the faith tradition of your family or that of your daughter's boyfriend that offers some basic counseling or classes in this regard. After all, if your daughter and this young man are willing to consider marriage, given their different backgrounds of Christian faith and culture, they should be willing to listen to the advice of other Christians. There is also the possibility of secular, non-Christian advice—which might represent a third-party, objective source.

3. As you note, the restrictions that your daughter is being asked to accept in terms of dress and grooming may not seem problematic to her now. The rose-colored glasses of romance and infatuation are motivating both her and the young man, but both of them should think long and hard about how she might feel about such restrictions when she is twenty-five or thirty. If she has regrets at some later date, whom might she blame? Will the marriage survive?

Has she been "free" long enough—is she old enough—to know what "freedom" is before she considers giving away so many personal decisions, handing them over to a church? Has she ever lived away from home? Has she been to college? Has she met enough young men to know the kind of person she is looking for?

4. There are many passages in the New Testament that govern cultural tastes and give Christians vast freedoms. Some churches and pastors seem to want to take those away. These passages make it clear that many decisions having to do with dress, alcohol consumption, grooming, music and art, whether Christians can go to movies, or whether Christians should dance, are up to us. To our own Master we stand or fall (Romans 14:4), not to some preacher or denomination. The books of Galatians and Colossians would be particularly helpful in such a study.

5. Of course, all of this is said within the dynamic that you as a parent must consider. As you well know, there are times when our protests and dogmatic advice will do nothing but strengthen the resolve of our children to do exactly the opposite. Your daughter is a young woman and, of course, you will need to be careful not to lecture, not to sermonize, not to threaten, but to strive to reach her in an adult-to-adult manner.

Do my husband and I need to attend the same church?

Q My husband and I are having problems with regard to which church we should attend. We both live in the same town where we grew up; however, we both still have membership in the different churches in which we were baptized. I currently sing in the choir, teach a Sunday school class, and serve in an administrative position at the church where I am a member.

My husband feels that we should be members of the same church. I occasionally attend the church of which he is a member, but when I am not in attendance at my church, I feel that I am not fulfilling my duties. My husband believes that I must adhere to his decision because I should obey my husband and we should become as one body. Please give us some direction. This has been a problem that we have discussed numerous times.

A Denominationalism can be a huge headache and a curse as it can separate Christians and cause "holy wars." At the same time, denominations can be helpful because they offer variety, speaking to us in our culture, giving us positive choices—choices that can make our Christian journey more enjoyable, understandable, and culturally relevant.

On the other hand, there are some churches that are not healthy. A choice of church is one to be made carefully, and any drawing of lines in the sand ought to also be made carefully. There are good reasons why some people stop attending one congregation, or one denomination, and start attending another. And, of course, people also change churches for inadequate reasons.

Ideally, for several reasons, families should be able to worship together. Many churches understand this need and make an effort to welcome family members who are not as comfortable in that particular congregation/denomination. But not all families do worship together, for a variety of reasons. There are many times when couples in situations like yours decide to leave their respective churches and choose a mutually acceptable church, new to both of them.

Is it okay to change churches?

Q *We have been attending a very small church for a few years now. We were introduced to the church shortly after we were married and have been attending ever since. The problem we are facing now is that the church no longer meets our needs. We have two children, ages one and four. The church offers no Sunday school or anything else for the children. They are forced to sit through the sermon quietly, not understanding anything about it. I have never understood the pastor, nor do I agree with all of his beliefs. Looking back, I would say that we only attended the church out of convenience. We made the decision to leave the church in search of another. However, we are close friends with people in the church and my in-laws attend this church. We have not been back to the church in over a month. When we are asked why we left the church, how should we respond without hurting anyone's feelings?*

A There are many reasons for beginning to attend a particular church, and there are many reasons for leaving. There is no reason why anyone should feel guilty or as if they are betraying God if they decide to move to another church.

29

A church needs to do two things in general:

1. Provide its parishioners and members with spiritual food and direction.

2. Give members an opportunity to participate and be involved in the life and activities of the church.

We all have a variety of needs, and some churches help us while others do not. It is possible for some people to go to a church and have that time be a huge test of their attitude, only to return home and take several days to "get over" church. In such a case, there is every reason to consider moving to another church.

Answers to those who ask us why we left? We may give a specific or vague response, or we may simply smile and respond that we felt that it was time to move to another church. After all, we may have left a church because we had a huge falling out with a leading family in the church, because we don't like the direction of church liturgy and music, or because we think the church is too controlling, too conservative, or too liberal. It may be that the pastor just isn't a good match for us—his sermons might be way too intellectual and boring. In your case, it seems you have serious questions about the pastor's beliefs. This alone is a valid reason to look for another fellowship. And there is no need to feel compelled to give exact and specific reasons to anyone about why you left.

If we are authentic Christians, our friendships with those who leave the church we continue to attend and support should remain intact. An exception might arise if they are joining some kind of unhealthy, biblically unbalanced church or even a cultic group that makes it almost impossible to continue being friends as they won't talk with us anymore. But merely to cease being friends because someone was once a Baptist and now becomes a Lutheran, or even less, simply moves to another Baptist church? We can confidently say that the God of the Bible is not pleased with withdrawing friendships when a brother or sister in Christ decides to move to another Christ-centered, well-balanced church.

The micromanaging pastor

Q *I have a difficult situation. Our church has a teaching pastor. He teaches straight from the Bible—no watered-down version, just the gospel. I hold the highest respect for him and realize that we are called to support our pastor. But he feels that he will be held accountable by God for His flock, so he makes all the decisions himself. I have brought this to his attention several times, but he does not believe it is a problem. We have no assistant pastor at this time, and we also have a Christian school, of which he is principal. He says that you can't force volunteers to work, so he ends up doing it all himself. When anyone disagrees, he considers it an attack from Satan. The church has stagnated, and we are not growing together. Some who wanted to grow have left the church and gone elsewhere. I just feel that if he delegated, or at least allowed open discussions, that we could serve the Lord to a fuller capacity. For one person to run everything seems cultic. I can't talk to anyone about this for feeling I am talking behind his back. Please help.*

A Thanks for your question. Some thoughts you may wish to consider:

1. You say, "We are called to support our pastor," yet such support should be within reason, and within other more important priorities. There are many qualifications and dis-

claimers to that statement; it is not an absolute. We may support those who lead us in the Lord as we are able, as other important priorities in our lives allow, and as we can in good conscience. If supporting our pastors is an absolute, then an unhealthy religious environment can result.

2. The idea that your pastor has to do everything himself, that he is always right, and that any opposition to him is an attack from Satan is a cause for concern. Wonderfully sincere men and women can be overcome by a sense of their own importance. If we are not careful, we can become legends in our own minds. We don't trust anyone else to do anything of importance because, well, because they just don't have the same insight, vision, wisdom, calling, anointing, yada yada yada. I know that mind-set, and it can be an oppressive, legalistic burden to everyone—not only the person who "bears the burden of leadership" (a phrase that is often used) but to everyone around him or her. One of the great principles to come out of the Protestant Reformation is the priesthood of all believers—the fact that we have all been called to ministry of some kind. Not all are pastors, but all are ministers, and all of God's children have contributions to make.

3. You speak of "stagnation." It is difficult to lead congregations, and it is difficult for congregations to grow. If everyone in every small congregation bailed out and headed down to the nearest mega-church, then the smaller churches of America would be in trouble (in fact, this very thing is happening!). This is not to say that there aren't times when we need to find a new church address. We are not compelled or expected by God to remain in an unhealthy or toxic environment. God does not expect us to endure an experience in church on Sunday that is so negative it takes us the rest of the

week to spiritually recover. So, if you stay, will you be able to help turn things around, or will you simply be getting into a deeper spiritual funk over that time? The church is not for the purpose of repressing us, but to "prepare God's people for works of service" (Ephesians 4:12). If it comes to a change, remember that there are many places and many ways for you to serve God, not just one geographical place or physical incorporation.

Finding a spiritual address where you belong

Q *I'm in a church I'm not sure I should be in. Although I have tried to find another one, I always end up coming back. I love the pastor and his teachings and wonder if that should be enough. I have a desire to be a part of the worship ministry, but the current worship pastor does not want to use me. I know God has given me a gift of singing. Because He chooses not to use me, I find myself envious of those He does use.*

I find myself sitting in the same pew week after week without making any real connections. The Bible study groups are mostly always filled with couples, and as a single person I feel out of place. The single people I meet already have their circle of friends and don't seem open to having me join in. Try as I might, I just can't seem to make friends. I really don't have any family either. I feel lonely, useless, and unloved. How do I find a place I belong with people who love me? I'm so afraid that God is disappointed with me because of the person I've become. In my heart, I know God is stripping me of everything to draw me closer to Him, but I'm afraid I'm not strong enough to surrender to Him. And I know until I do, this will be my life.

A   The church should be a place for us to find expression
of our gifts and talents—for, as the Reformation teaching tells us, we are, as the body of Christ, a priesthood of believers. You are not feeling needed, used, or helpful. Therefore,
your church may not be the place for you. I cannot make an
absolute determination, but it seems there might be a better
spiritual address for you. All of us as Christians can and do
occasionally feel lost, alone, and unsure in church, but we need
not feel this way on an ongoing basis.

Your gift of music and singing should not be ignored. It
seems to be something God has given you, and you want to
use it to His glory. If you cannot use your talent in your
church, then you should feel free to find somewhere you can.
You might even remain a member of your church and use
your gift elsewhere, but it might also mean that you will join
another church in order to effectively use and share your gift
with others.

Your desire to be in a place that ministers to you, that does
not make you feel awkward as a single person, is not wrong; it
is not selfish. You need ministry, and you need friendship. One
of the reasons we have many differing churches, congregations,
and ministries is that no one church, congregation, or ministry
can help everyone. No imperfect place can be the perfect place
for everyone. Perhaps you need to replace the church you are
now attending with a more single-friendly church.

God is not disappointed with the person you have
become. He may, in large part, be involved in nudging you
into another part of His body—another place. He wants to use
you, and He wants to minister to you. He wants to fill you and
satisfy you while also involving you in service. He wants the
same thing for all of us as His children. That "place" doesn't

always drop into our laps, so you may need to d̶
ing and networking.

If you decide to change your spiritual address, ̶ ̶ ̶
please—exchange a relatively healthy and Christ-centered environment for one that seems to offer opportunity for involvement
and service but is not centered in Jesus Christ. Don't exchange
a healthy spiritual environment for an unhealthy or abusive
one merely for the purpose of having your talents seemingly
recognized and used.

We do not, as Christians, find our primary happiness in
things, but in Jesus. We find our happiness in giving ourselves to
Him, in participating with Him in a cause and effort that is not
about us, but about others. If your church doesn't offer you a
way to reach out, why not consider volunteering at a homeless
shelter, at a soup kitchen, at a seniors' home where you can sing,
in an effort to send care packages to soldiers overseas, in a distri-
bution of toys to inner-city youth? Lose yourself in service to
Christ and to His little ones. Such activities will not only help
you make it through lonely times but will also help you to focus
on what is real as opposed to what is surface and shallow.

No shirt, no shoes, no services

Q *Our pastor recently made an announcement in our
church bulletin concerning the "dress code" for church
and church functions. The bulletin states: "No shorts, no pants for
females, no sloppy jeans, no midriffs, no Bermudas, no shirts with
distasteful pictures, art, or language. Wear your best to the Lord's
house." Is he being fair to the church, or is he crossing the line? I
thought that it didn't really matter what you had on as long as you
came to church to worship God and learn about His Word.*

A There is nothing unbiblical about the ability or even the responsibility of a school, a family, a church, or a workplace to set reasonable standards of dress and grooming codes. I see no biblical disagreement with a common-sense, balanced, and moderate use of such authority.

Parents are in charge of their homes. Parents may insist that children sit down at the table to eat. They may insist that children always wash their hands before meals. They may insist that children "endure" family conversation and may not leave the table until they ask to be excused. I personally see nothing onerous about such regulations. If, on the other hand, parents insisted that children sit at the table for one hour before meals and one hour after, in silence, or that children dress in their "Sunday best" for every family meal—then in most homes, and most Western cultures, that would probably be excessive and may, in the words of the apostle Paul, be "exasperating our children" (see Ephesians 6:4).

As for formal church services, there is something to be said for dress and grooming—but not with such authoritarian claims that dress itself is of such importance that one's relationship with God is affected. Denominations and congregations differ on this issue. For example, when I am asked to preach at a congregation I have never visited and no one specifically informs me of appropriate dress (especially for a minister), I will usually wear a tie. I actually prefer to preach in a nice, casual shirt with no tie, but I will gladly wear one if what I am wearing will become an obstacle to others hearing the message.

In terms of attending services, I enjoy attending a church which invites and "allows" me to wear slacks and a sports shirt, without a tie. If I were not wearing a tie and a pastor made a dogmatic statement that men must wear ties to church, I would not agree—and I would then have to find other compelling reasons to continue attending that church while wearing a tie. (Perhaps the fact that my wife enjoyed that church or that my children or grandchildren enjoyed the church might be factors that would tip the scales.) Still, I would worry that the excessive use of authority on such a minimalistic issue might reoccur at other times and with other issues, and I don't believe that authoritarianism is a good match for the gospel of Jesus Christ.

I believe that clothing worn while worshipping God should be clean and not grungy. When it comes to teens, I believe the church should show some latitude, given the culture in which they live. On the other hand, there is something to be said for the idea that going to church is a little different than going to the supermarket or stepping out the back door to mow the lawn.

Rethinking church

Q *I've been rethinking my whole church scene. I enjoy church for what it provides. I like to see friends, I like to hear a good message, and I enjoy Christian music and hymns. But for me, church has not been a God-encounter. In fact, outside of church and any of its activities and programs, I am finding people in my life who inspire me and encourage me to dig deeper, and I like to think that I am doing some of that same kind of thing for others. The whole concept of not being concerned about where exactly I attend church and how often I physically show up inside of a building is new to me, but I am coming to believe that each one of us is a walking, talking 24/7 church.*

A You seem to be discovering the difference between *the* church and *a* church. It's a distinction that can make some uncomfortable, for it suggests that *the* church is bigger than they can imagine, and beyond their ability to measure and quantify. We can easily confuse the fact that our relationship with other humans, particularly in a group that is organized for the purpose of being *a* healthy and vibrant part of *the* body of Christ on earth, is the defining element of our Christianity. *The* church is the spiritual body of Christ on earth. *The* church, *the* body of Christ, is universal; it defies legally incorporated boundaries and doctrinal definitions. *The* church is wherever God wants it to be; part of it is known and visible to us, but most of it is not. We can and do know other Christians, but the vast majority of folks who are part of *the* universal body of Christ are unknown to us.

We are placed in *the* body of Christ by virtue of our acceptance of God's gracious offer of His love and His grace. When we accept Jesus Christ as our Savior, we begin an eternal, personal, and intimate relationship with God, and we become a part of *the* church. As part of *the* church, we determine how and when we might gather together, in community, with others who are also a part of *the* church. Sometimes we do that in a building with four walls; sometimes we do that in other ways. When one is part of *the* church, there are many ways to *do* church.

We may be members of *the* church without being members of *a* church, even though *a* church may insist that we cannot do so. *A* church may tell us that if we are simply members of *the* church, we are missing something and might even be "left behind"! But the ongoing belief of *the* church of Jesus Christ over the centuries has been that our relationship with *a* church is of far less importance than our relationship with *the* church.

Jesus did not speak of *the* church as a place to go but rather as a living relationship to and with Him and with those who share that relationship—our brothers and sisters in *the* universal body of Christ. *The* church is something we are, far more than *a* place we go. Having a perfect attendance record at *a* church is not the goal of our Christian journey.

If and when our relationship with a specific group of people that gathers together in *a* particular building in *a* specific geographical location ends, our relationship with God continues. We are still part of *the* church. It can be a spiritual tightrope act to avoid attaching your primary spiritual identity with *a* geographically located church. It can also be a spiritual tightrope act to be an active part of *the* church without being a part of *a* church.

There are people who once joined *a* church after God placed them in *the* church, but their relationship with *a* church (or several individual churches for that matter) turned out to be a nightmare. Some are worried that their relationship with God is not what it should be because they are not in *a* church, but they honestly cannot bring themselves, at least at this time, to be part of another geographically located, brick-and-mortar church. They should realize that they are in *the* church, and their relationship with God is secure and safe.

Some say that we need to be part of *a* church so that we can fellowship with others. But our fellowship is primarily with Jesus, the head of *the* church, and we may fellowship with others without being in *a* church (1 John 1:3). Others warn that we can't survive spiritually without the "covering of the body," which is a religious innovation meaning that we will be spiritual chopped liver if we don't show up on Sunday morning to watch a praise-and-worship concert, or, alternatively, be dragged kicking and screaming over the hot coals of hell.

There are many ways for us to be a part of *the* church in its physical manifestations in our world, culture, and society. There are many ways for us to be involved, to give, to participate, and to share with others the relationship that we have been given by God's grace. One way is to be a part of *a* healthy, Christ-centered, well-balanced church. If *a* church is healthy, they will not make inordinate and unbiblical demands of us, such as 10 percent tithing, perfect attendance, oppressive demands, and intrusions into our life outside of *a* church.

There is a place for *a* church, and there definitely is a place for *the* church. *The* church is eternal, but there will be a time when there is no need for *a* church, for the Lord God Almighty and the Lamb will be *the* temple of the new Jerusalem (Revelation 21:22). Sometimes *a* church works together in concert with *the* church, and sometimes *a* church doesn't. *The* church and *the* church alone can supply the spiritual intimacy that God gives to His children. *A* church can help and assist and complement what *the* church provides; sometimes *a* church does and sometimes *a* church does not. There is nothing spiritually wrong, inferior, or substandard with a child of God being in *the* church without maintaining membership in *a* church.

FAITH

Will God bless me for making a financial vow?

Q *I watched a television ministry that claims if you make a financial vow unto the Lord, it will change your circumstances. When you're seeking answers, you just want to believe that something will work, almost like looking for a sign. I want to have faith in God, but at times I'm tempted to transfer my faith to human promises.*

A The program you watched may base its "theology" in the Word-Faith movement, which, among other unbiblical teachings, teaches the health-wealth or Prosperity Gospel. The teaching is based upon human effort and performance. Obey, and you will be blessed; disobey, and you will be cursed.

But the gospel of Jesus Christ is not a "you do this and then I will respond and do that" message. The New Covenant God offers to us is not a covenant of physical prosperity, but instead a covenant of adversity. We are asked to take up our cross and follow Him, to present our bodies as living sacrifices, to serve others rather than ourselves, and to think of the needs of others as equal to our own.

Some Word-Faith teachers seem to promise the moon to

41

people who are in desperate straits in terms of finances and health. These poor and sick people have no hope, and Word-Faith preaching holds it out—in exchange for the little money these people have. God does not work that way. God's grace is absolutely free. Paul calls it the riches of God's grace. God's promises to us are far more focused on the spiritual and eternal rather than the here and now. For that reason, many who will be called great in the kingdom will have been the least here on earth. The parable of Lazarus and the rich man teaches us that.

Don't be taken in by false teaching, however attractive it may sound. The authentic gospel of Jesus Christ is not proclaimed by infomercial-like programs where people wave money and promise cars and new houses to those who simply buy their tapes for six easy payments of $19.95 or make a "love gift" of more than $100.

Will my doubts cause me to lose my faith?

Q I have accepted Christ and been baptized, but I worry one day something might affect my faith. I do not have enough faith whenever I face difficulties in life. Will I lose my salvation if I have so many doubts about God when I face difficulties? I am only twenty-eight years old. How can I be certain that God is always with me?

A Here are several thoughts to keep in mind:
1. God loves you today as much as He did yesterday, and He will still love you that much tomorrow. He will never love you more than He does right now. He is in the business of saving us, not destroying us. He is not mad at or with you.
2. No human has "enough" faith—not ever. Our faith is

imperfect, fickle, and inadequate. That's why we need, and why we are offered, the faith of Jesus Christ. He will fill us with His faith as He lives His life within us.

3. You will not lose your salvation because you have doubts or because you are depressed. God does not give us eternal life only to take it away when we fail to please Him. He does not give only to take away.

It is difficult for humans to be convinced that God is always with us and that our status as one of His children is unchanged. We live in a world of conditional love and acceptance. In human cultures, others like us, accept us, and love us when we do things that please them. But God is not a human, and He does not treat us in a conditional manner. His love is unconditional, and because we are humans that kind of love is hard to understand. However, simply because God's love is difficult to understand does not mean it is not real. A cow may not understand how to use a computer, but that does not mean the computer is not real. We worship and revere and love God because He is bigger, better, superior, greater, and more loving, just, and merciful than we are. We worship God because He is not like we are! And we can thank Him and be forever grateful that He is not like us!

What is faith?

Q *I am a Christian but still have a problem understanding what faith is. Could you elaborate for me?*

A Faith, in brief, is a belief in and commitment to something or someone (for a Christian, that would be Someone). Christians have complete faith and trust in Jesus

Christ, that He was and is who He claimed, that He did what He said, and that what He did is sufficient and complete for our salvation. Apart from God, we are humanly incapable of expressing this trust in God, so the faith we have to believe in God is itself a gift of God. Faith is the basis of our relationship with God.

What is "blind faith"?

Q *What exactly is "blind faith"? I have a friend who contends that faith in God has to be "blind" because you can't physically see God. I can't "see" the wind, but I know it's there. I hope you understand what I am trying to ask.*

A The term "blind faith" can be an oxymoron (two words that are mutually self-contradictory). The term "blind faith" is often used for emphasis, to contrast blind faith with biblical faith, to help us understand that biblical faith is based upon evidence, that biblical faith does not "come out of the blue."

Faith, according to the Bible, is "being sure of what we hope for and certain of what we do not see" (Hebrews 11:1). The "do not see" part leads to the use of the word *blind* at times. But the use of the term "blind faith" is usually negative, about faith that has no grounding, no rationale, and no basis in fact or history. Biblical faith, given that context, is not blind.

Faith, Paul tells us, "comes from hearing the message [of the gospel], and the message is heard through the word of Christ" (Romans 10:17). Faith, the Bible tells us, is a gift. We do not conjure up faith. We do not wish for it. We do not decide that we will have faith tomorrow when today we have none.

The disciples asked Jesus to "increase" their faith (Luke

17:5). They had the idea, as humans always have, that faith is like a commodity, that we can go to a heavenly grocery store or spiritual gas station and get more. But faith is not quantified, and we certainly are not judged by God or rewarded (or not rewarded) because we either have enough faith or insufficient faith. In one sense, our faith can be said to "increase" as we grow in Christ, for the more we are in Christ and the more closely we walk with God, the more faithful we will be. But the idea of "increasing our faith" is simply a description of what God is doing in us; because at the end of it all, faith is a gift from God.

PROTESTS AND PLACARDS

Should Christians boycott and protest?

Q *Should Christians boycott? Should they actively use their "dollar power" to support or protest moral issues?*

A This is a difficult question, and I don't know that there is one right or wrong answer for it. I do know that there are many boycotts Christians have organized in the past that have not worked. In fact, some of these protests have boomeranged and allowed or caused Christians to be seen as silly and perhaps even as hateful. The Southern Baptists decided, some years ago, to boycott Disney, Disney World, and Disneyland because Disney had decided to extend health and other employee benefits to the partners of employees who lived in homosexual relationships. From all reports, the protest/boycott did not diminish the financial success of Disney. Apparently, it wasn't even successful in keeping Baptists and their children away from Disney and its products. The flipside of this protest is that it was used to paint Christians as hateful and mean-spirited people.

Some churches and ministries seem to do little more than

"take a stand." Among such groups, it seems that virtually every month there is some new position that needs to be taken, some new boycott or protest. At the same time, some of these churches and ministries become politically polarized. After a while, if one listens to and reads about their message and mission, it seems much closer to a political action committee than it does to the gospel of Jesus Christ. There is a ministry whose efforts and work I once enjoyed, but over time their mission became so politically polarized and seemingly vindictive that I have little in common with them now.

Having said this, I don't mean to say that there isn't a time for Christians to make a difference. Christians should exercise their right to vote, to organize as a group, and to influence legislators to pass laws that are in sync with the kingdom of God. However, when we do boycott, let's make the lines we draw count for something. Let us voice our feelings about issues that are critically important, and let us ask how our protests will help us reflect the light of Jesus.

HEAVEN

Going directly to heaven?

Q *In our prayer group, we were discussing the afterlife. Some say that we go directly to heaven to be at the Father's side, and others are saying that we are asleep in heaven until the Second Coming. What are your feelings on this matter? It seems to me that Scripture says both.*

A The Bible says that when we die we are absent from the body but present with the Lord. This is a "time" (eternity is not measured by clocks and calendars) that is called the *intermediate state*. The intermediate state is when our bodies are dead, our souls/spirits are with God before the second coming of Jesus, when our bodies are resurrected to immortal life. We often speak of the intermediate state as going "to" heaven. But heaven is not a place; heaven is wherever God is. Where is God? He is omnipresent. He is everywhere. That means He is not somewhere at the expense of failing to be present elsewhere.

Is this heaven of the intermediate state different than the heaven of the new heavens and new earth described in the book of Revelation? Yes, it would seem so. The intermediate heaven is a "place" where we are not yet reunited with our immortal bodies, and it is not yet the new heaven and new earth.

In the intermediate state, are we "sleeping" (unconscious) or are we conscious? Most Christians throughout history, as well as most biblical indicators, would say that we are conscious while in the intermediate heaven. A few believe in what is called "soul sleep" because they misunderstand one of the biblical usages of the word *sleep*. In some contexts, sleep is used as a metaphor for death (for example, "David slept with his fathers" [1 Kings 2:10, KJV]). But when the word *sleep* is used as a metaphor for death, it is not describing a literal state of the soul while in intermediate heaven.

Just how big is heaven?

Q *I recently heard a sermon about heaven. The preacher said heaven was shaped like a pyramid. According to him, the light in heaven would cast shadows. He even had measurements for the size of heaven. It had floors, ceilings, and walls. It was an interesting topic, but I am skeptical. Is any of this biblically based? Is it just someone's attempt to explain the unexplainable based on physics or some other man-made ideology?*

A Heaven is a "place" that has no physical boundaries, since heaven is where God is—and God is outside of time and space. He is uncreated, holy, perfect, and eternal, not subject to the limitations of humanity. Therefore heaven is not "shaped," nor does it have "measurements." It has no floors, ceilings, or walls. Perhaps the pastor knows this and was trying to make the topic understandable, but at the very best there should have been some disclaimer so that the audience knew that eternity is not at all like the world of time and space we inhabit.

HELL

If you don't accept Christ, will you go to hell?

Q *The church I attend says if a person doesn't accept Christ in this lifetime, they will go to be tortured in an ever-burning, eternal hell. I do not believe that. Where do they find that in the Bible?*

A This topic is one of the "hot" buttons within Christendom. Many believe that hell must be regularly and dogmatically preached, that people's feet must be held over the ever-burning coals of hell to motivate them to obey God. As a general rule, the more rules and regulations are the center of preaching and teaching, the hotter the hell that is preached. However, while the Bible seems to teach that hell and heaven either exist now or will exist, the religious definitions and descriptions of heaven and hell differ widely with those of the Bible.

Within Christendom, the popular stereotype of hell was forever changed by Dante's *Divine Comedy*. Dante proposed different levels of hell, differing intensities of eternal torment based on the gravity of the sin being punished. Many Christians, both professional pastors and teachers, as well as laity, take their clues about hell from this outdated, outmoded, unscientific, and decidedly un-Christlike view of hell from the religious heritage of Dante.

Many religious folks believe that hell must be preached so that Christians will "keep in line." But when one carefully considers what the gospel of Jesus Christ is all about, what God's grace actually means, and how it plays out in our lives, keeping people under religious control is not the desire of Jesus Christ.

Hell is vigorously defended by many, and anyone who would beg to differ is often labeled a libertine, permissive, a crank, a heretic, or all of the above. A careful examination of the Bible, the nature of God, and the nature of the gospel of Jesus Christ is often not the foundation of such heated exchanges. The real issue for religious legalism is the defense of its arsenal, the defense of this religious club that it can use to keep people in line.

Sadly, such manipulative teaching is not only unbiblical, it doesn't work. People are waking up to the abuse and torture of Scripture that has been going on. The fiery sinners-in-the-hands-of-an-angry-God stuff is more religious than it is Christian.

Having said that, do I believe in heaven and hell? I believe heaven is eternity spent in the presence of God, and hell is eternity spent apart from God. That's it. That is not enough, obviously, for some within Christendom who feel they need fiery tirades and yelling matches to keep people from doing bad things. Keeping people from doing bad things is a noble and necessary goal, and we can all wish that more parents, teachers, pastors, and others could do more to make this world a better place. But the goal of keeping people in line does not justify the means of fear religion. There isn't enough dogmatic and specific information in the Bible to help us define the exactness of hell. There is in Dante, but last time I checked, Dante's *Divine Comedy* is not one of the books of the Bible.

Who goes to hell (or heaven), what the criteria is, how many people are or will be in hell and heaven, etc.—these are often religious devices. Some churches basically teach, while many others carefully but strongly suggest, that heaven will essentially be confined to their little congregation or denomination and all other riffraff will be assigned a less-favorable eternal destination. Many teach that hell is reserved for those who don't see it their way, who don't quite measure up to their religious standards. But God says that salvation is by grace, and that He alone determines how and when the riches of His grace are given.

MARRIAGE

Will God recognize my marriage without a license and ceremony?

Q *When is a marriage recognized by God? Does He recognize a marriage that takes place in the hearts of two people before the public ceremony? My boyfriend and I made a commitment to each other in my living room one evening, and I was under the belief we were married but without the public ceremony. I was hesitant to legally marry him at the time because I wanted to get out of debt before legally binding him to my debt. I told him I needed about a year to do so.*

A The very kind of situation you describe is the reason that governments do not allow citizens to subjectively determine what constitutes marriage. God allows, expects, and, beyond that, actually ordains governments to make civil laws and enforce them. Marriage is governed by the laws of the state. Without such laws, we would have anarchy with claims of marriage and family having no objective.

Marriage, therefore, by government regulations, must involve a ceremony—a formal declaration by two people to accept responsibility for financial debts that the new partnership will incur.

It is true that a marriage is between two humans and God—and no one else. But we are imperfect humans, and we need contracts that bind us, which is the place of civil governments. Governments do not generally require clergy, but they require a license and a binding contract. They require a similar thing for divorce and remarriage. Without such requirements, multiple marriages and polygamous marriages would be common.

Your statement about hesitation to be married because of financial debts is a *de facto* proof that marriage, undertaken properly, with a license and approval by the state, is a business relationship, among other things.

Marriage is a public declaration of the commitment of two people, publicly declared so that all others—family, friends, and strangers—know of the unique status of the man and woman who have made a commitment to each other.

Does God allow divorce?

Q *What does the Bible say about divorce and remarriage?*

A The Bible makes it very clear—God hates divorce. Marriage should be "till death do us part." But, because we are imperfect, we humans often fall short of what God intends, and the statistics in our society bear this out.

How Christians view what God says about divorce usually depends upon what is called the exception clause in the Gospels, a clause that is interpreted in many ways. Matthew 19:9 tells us divorce should not take place "except for marital unfaithfulness." The Greek word *porneia* translated as "marital unfaithfulness" can be interpreted in several ways.

Those who are contemplating marriage after divorce lean generally toward a wider allowance of what "marital unfaithfulness" means, for obvious reasons. Those who are extremely strict about remarriage after divorce believe that marital unfaithfulness on the part of the offending spouse must be prolonged and continual before any remarriage can be biblically "allowed" under these instructions. This perspective can also owe more to human ideas than divine wisdom. There are a variety of opinions across the denominational spectrum.

Why was polygamy allowed in the Old Testament?

Q *Why did Abraham and other biblical patriarchs have multiple wives? Was this a common practice at the time and not disdained as it is today? How did God view such marriages? I'm not looking for an endorsement of polygamy; I just don't understand why it was commonplace in the Old Testament.*

A From the beginning, God made it clear that the standard for humans was monogamy. Adam and Eve, in the beginning, set this pattern (see Genesis 1:27; 2:21–25). Throughout the Old Testament, God warned men in that patriarchal society not to "multiply wives." The Law of Moses includes such a prohibition (Deuteronomy 17:17).

Jesus reaffirms this standard in Matthew 19:4—one male and one female defines marriage. Paul says the same in 1 Corinthians 7:2. Ephesians 5 tells us that the relationship between Christ and the church, His bride, is monogamous. God reveals Himself to us as one God, and the Judeo-Christian tradition insists on monotheism.

God never established, founded, blessed, or commanded polygamy. A study of the polygamists in the Old Testament (such as Abraham, Jacob, and David) will reveal that they all paid dearly with hurt and pain experienced by their families. Simply because people whose lives are recorded in the Bible engaged in a particular practice or behavior does not mean that by recording that behavior God is endorsing it.

Can a Catholic and a Southern Baptist find happiness together?

Q *I have a boyfriend who is a Christian in the Catholic church, and I am a Christian in a Southern Baptist church. We have been talking a lot about marriage, but we don't want to go through with it until we decide which church to go to because we want to go to church as a family. I believe we are both Christians, but I don't agree with some of the Catholic church's traditions, such as confession and baptizing of babies. Are there scriptural backgrounds for these things?*

A There are a number of major differences that can undermine a marital relationship; among them are: 1) cultural differences, 2) age differences, 3) family acceptance or rejection of a potential spouse, 4) racial differences, and 5) religious differences. You are wise to discuss differences in your denominational views now. Sometimes religious differences between a couple are not really that major, but real problems can come from their respective families who insist upon particular religious forms, ceremonies, and rituals. The movie *My Big Fat Greek Wedding* provides a hilarious depiction of this very thing. There are differences that the couple and their families agree to smooth over for a few years. But when children arrive, major conflicts can arise.

I don't have any easy answers here. For this very reason, many marry only fellow Baptists or fellow Catholics because it would be too hard, perhaps even impossible, to integrate a potential spouse into their religious/cultural/family world.

One compromise that many couples have agreed upon is to find a healthy, well-balanced, Christ-centered church—sometimes a nondenominational church—that offends neither of their faith traditions too much and might represent a compromise on some. This avenue is hard work because there is a chance of upsetting not only one family but both. But one thing that parents must realize (I speak from some experience because my wife and I have two married children and four grandchildren) is that when your adult children marry, they really do need their own lives. It takes some parents a while to realize this. Sadly, some never get it.

If two people decide to start attending a third, mutually acceptable church and to leave their former churches behind, there will be some church shopping involved. I know of couples who have made such a decision but who have realized they may not find such a church until after they have married. Thus the decision remains about which church to be married in. Of course, this very pressure is why some couples have simply eloped.

It is possible for two Christians to be happily married and still have differing faith traditions. They must agree before the marriage that their love for one another will transcend any religious or denominational permutation of Christianity and to respect each other's views for as long as they both may live.

Will God send me a spouse?

Q *I have a couple of friends who do not believe in dating. Actually, they believe that the Lord will miraculously send them a spouse. My question: is there such a thing as God sending someone a spouse if that person does not date? And if so, how do you know that person is the one?*

A Courtship has taken a variety of forms throughout time. Few people today would be comfortable with the practice in Genesis when patriarchs virtually chose a mate for their child.

"The Lord will send a spouse"—what does that mean? Will the Lord send me a graduate degree, will He send me a house or apartment to live in, or will He send me a car to drive? Sometimes Christians become naïve about what God will do (and not do), and some of their assumptions, in God's name, border on superstition.

There are times when people say that the Lord told them to do something, when the Lord may not have "said" or urged them to do that thing at all. They are simply attributing their selfish desires to God and seeking to justify what they want to do by claiming that God is directing them to do exactly what they want to do. I find it amazing that God agrees with so many people, so often, about exactly what they have already subjectively determined to do.

Back to your question—can the Lord send someone a spouse if that someone does not believe in the courtship "ritual" we today call dating? Of course He can. Has he? Of course He has. The Bible gives examples.

But perhaps that begs your question, which seems to be,

how much can we or should we sit back and wait for God to make something happen in our lives, and how much should we "take matters into our own hands" or at least do something?

There's an old joke: A man was poor and blamed God. He told God that he had prayed for twenty years, pleading with God to let him win the lottery. God said, "Yes, I heard your prayers, but you know what? You never even purchased one lottery ticket."

In case you are offended that I should mention the lottery, I don't use this story as a commentary about whether God is happy or unhappy if we buy a lottery ticket. It's a story with a point. Of course God has a plan for our lives, and of course God answers prayers (perhaps not always with the yes we expect). But is there anything that we can do? Is "doing something" a lack of faith? Isn't it better to get off our backsides and at least head in some direction, doing something, even if that something and that direction is wrong and needs to be corrected later, than to simply sit around and wait for God to part the waters of the Red Sea for us?

I believe that we are saved by grace, that nothing we do can contribute to our salvation. However, I also believe that God wants us to be active, to seek ways to improve our lot in life, to volunteer to help others, to be going somewhere with our lives.

PRAYER

Is the "Sinner's Prayer" required for salvation?

Q *Some people told me that God does not hear our prayers until we say what is called a "Sinner's Prayer." Recently, a friend told me that she believes God does not hear her prayers because she does not regularly attend church and because she had not said the "Sinner's Prayer." I disagreed with her and told her that God loves her. Later, she let me know that a preacher where she goes to church would be glad to talk with me about the "Sinner's Prayer" and explain it to me. I need some insight before I talk to him.*

A The "Sinner's Prayer" is just another sincere attempt to forge some instrument or device that will help proclaim the gospel. It's a suggested prayer designed to help people see their need of God. It is neither virtuous nor evil, right or wrong, of and by itself. The "Sinner's Prayer" is not sacred. It might be "a" tool to help some, but it is certainly not the only tool. I believe that we can dogmatically say that many have been saved without ever saying the "Sinner's Prayer."

Nothing in the Bible suggests that God limits Himself to hearing the prayers of those who regularly attend church, or a specific church. Thank God! The idea of any human explaining to another why God hasn't/doesn't/won't answer prayers is religiosity at its worst. God makes the sun to shine and the rain to fall on the righteous and the unrighteous (Matthew 5:45).

What is the point of prayer?

Q *What exactly is the point of prayer? I understand that in the New Testament it says we are to "pray continually," but I have also heard that God is going to do His will no matter what anyway, so what would be the point in asking for things? Can we change the mind of God if we put our requests before Him such as a child can do with their parents (providing they would not harm us)? Is it possible to change the will of God by praying for another situation other than the one we are in? Wouldn't circumstances happen anyway even if we did not pray for them?*

A Statements you make in your question lead to the answer. The purpose of prayer is not to change God. That is a misconception that mere humans have. Many believe, sometimes aided and abetted by religions, notions, rituals, and ceremonies, that we can manipulate God, that we can bargain with Him. We believe that our actions can influence Him to do what we want.

Prayer is a way/time for us to communicate with the holy and sovereign God. It is not a tool for us to use in an attempt to change the holy and perfect God, who, of course, does not need to change. Prayer is actually a way/time for God to change our hearts.

God invites us to spend time with Him in prayer. God invites us to share our concerns and requests with Him. He offers us an intimate relationship, and in a relationship, real, heartfelt, soul-baring communication takes place. Prayer should not be viewed primarily as a time when we have a battle of wills with God.

Won't what God wants to happen, happen anyway, whether we pray or not? What if all children had such a relationship with their parents, or all spouses with each other? No need to talk, discuss, debate, reason, laugh, or cry together. *Que sera sera.* It will all happen anyway, so why utter a single word? Again, prayer is a way to experience God, to enjoy Him, to come to know Him, a time and a tool for Him to change, mold, and shape us.

MOVIES, BEER, AND
ROCK 'N' ROLL

Can Christians party?

Q *I have Christian friends who drink beer and wine, enjoy music, and go to concerts, plays, and movies. Much of this artistic expression, as well as lyrics to rock music, is so full of sex and drugs. Paul said not to conform to the ways of the world. I don't want to be self-righteous, but I question the salvation of such people.*

A I may be a person somewhat like the ones you describe. I have a beer several times a month, and perhaps a glass of wine several times a week. Last time I checked, Jesus created wine, lots of it. The Bible does not condemn alcohol; it condemns its abuse. While alcohol can become addictive, there are no biblical prohibitions about its use, certainly not the way some churches imply. Consuming or not consuming alcohol, in moderation, is not the acid test of Christianity. Christians should not be under any pressure to imbibe or to refrain. They may have excellent reasons for doing either. Being an alcoholic is, of course, reason to completely refrain. There are also health reasons for refraining, and according to some reports there may be health reasons for taking a little red wine on a regular basis. The Bible does have something to say about our insisting that others follow our specific lifestyles, and that unless they do, they are, at the very least, inferior Christians.

Rock music? No question. I enjoy it. I like U2, the Eagles, Fleetwood Mac, and many others. My freedom in Christ means that I can also enjoy Christian contemporary, classic Christian hymns, gospel, jazz, classical, country, reggae, blues, and even polka (but only after I have had either beer or wine!). My personal taste does, of course, not define authentic Christianity, but you didn't ask about Christianity; you described Christians with whom you take exception.

Having said that, I have not addressed your issue about lyrics in rock music. It seems to many that contemporary music, alternative and rap, for example, have more sex, drugs, and violence references than earlier eras. On the other hand, there are lyrics from the Roaring Twenties that were X-rated, along with jazz and blues that go back more than one hundred years. Going beyond that, if one studies the history of literature, poetry, art—as well as music—there has always been a component of such artistic expression that was pagan and immoral.

We can throw it all out—all music, all dancing, all movies, all TV, all Internet (for it is filled with porn as well)—or we can carefully discriminate and wisely use art, artistic expression, and technology in a Christ-centered way. The Bible is filled with poetry and lyrical expression. David, a man after God's heart, was a deeply gifted, artistically expressive man, and he was criticized for his dancing. (I have been too, but for completely different reasons!)

It seems to me that we can draw a narrow circle around our family, our church, and ourselves in an attempt to keep the world out, or we can realize that "the world" is everywhere. We can never draw a tight-enough circle to keep all the sin out, and therefore we should understand that our culture is not necessarily an enemy. It is a force to be reckoned with, used, monitored, and even redeemed.

There are issues that we as Christians don't tolerate. For example, there is no such thing as murder in moderation. There is no such thing as a little bit of stealing, lying, gossip, lust, and pride being okay "as long as it doesn't become excessive." But there are other areas that demand some careful thought. There have been many eras and generations of Christians who effectively threw out, sealed, or allegorized away the meaning of the Song of Solomon. It is a song of married love and was simply too scandalous for some. Other passages in the Old Testament that are explicit in terms of sex and/or violence have been viewed in a similar way. Such biblical passages are not suitable for a first-grade Sunday school class, but they are written for our admonition and our example, for all Scripture is inspired. While some biblical passages would not be appropriate for six-year-olds, they might be for sixteen-year-olds and certainly are for adults.

I am a firm believer in God's grace because of the particular religious swamp I was in for thirty-five years. When Jesus rescued me, I started to look around, and while I was dismayed at the stuff I had believed, practiced, and preached, I also found that there were many other forms of legalism that thrive in God's name. Consequently, as a result of God's grace, it is my belief that we often become, in our desire to do the right thing, far more restrictive, authoritarian, and controlling than Jesus.

When I speak of God's grace, some dismiss me as a libertine, as someone who is trying to find ways to justify sinful behavior. I find that such a response is the only way that the human mind can deal with the lavish and extravagant grace of God, grace, and love that is far beyond our wildest imagination. God loves us, that I know. God is not mad at us, that I know. God does not specialize in long laundry lists of dos and don'ts in the way that many religions do. God instead works within us, Jesus lives in us, so that the life we lead in this flesh is not the life we once led. Fear, oppression, and religious control do not characterize the authentic new life of our risen Lord.

Jesus is my Lord. I am free in Him (Galatians 5:1) from anyone who would attempt to impose extra-biblical teachings or traditions or requirements on me. And so are you. I pray that God will open your heart to the good news of the gospel, the gospel of Jesus Christ that has nothing to do with doing as we please, but has everything to do with Jesus doing as He pleases in our lives.

GRACE

Law or grace—a debate

Q1 *I have read repeatedly in the Bible about the "wedding garment"—most importantly, the passage where the man in heaven is seated at the table of the feast and is found not to have a wedding garment on. He is asked why and is speechless. So he is bound and thrown into "the darkness, where there will be weeping and gnashing of teeth" (Matthew 22:13). How do I know if I will have a "wedding garment"?*

A1 Great question! A study of wedding garments in the New Testament reveals that only Jesus can provide the wedding garment. The wedding garment is given by grace, not earned by works. No amount of sewing or shopping on our part can provide the wedding garment that is needed for being seated at the Lord's table. He alone can provide that garment, and He does for those who accept Him as sufficient and able to do for them what they cannot do for themselves.

Q2 *That's not the point. You see, this man had already been raptured up into heaven and had been accepted with the Lord's host of saints. How then could he suddenly be found lacking in this one thing?*

A2 The point I made, according to the gospel of Jesus Christ, is the point. You are telling me that this man in Matthew 22:1–14 who had no wedding garment had been raptured into heaven only to be found lacking? How do you come to such an interpretation? Nothing in this passage suggests such a thing. The answer to your dilemma lies in looking at this parable without the impediment of what you think it says. If you think it teaches what you already believe to be true, then to you it will still seem to teach such things after you examine it. I suggest you start with a study of parables, to find out whether they supply exact time settings such as you are insisting upon for this parable.

Q3 *It's my salvation in question here. Can you think of any other hypothetical wedding feast that would occur before the Second Coming? I place the wedding feast as occurring after the Second Coming. I find 2 Peter 1:1–10 as setting the standard for the wedding garment. This wedding parable in Matthew 22 says someone can be in heaven after the Second Coming lacking a wedding garment. That is frightening to me, because I fear that I am lacking. That passage in 2 Peter is a lot to live up to. Peter says, "Make your calling and election sure" (2 Peter 1:10), and Jesus said, "For many are invited, but few are chosen" (Matthew 22:14). I feel that I am being told here to make my calling and election sure when someone can still be cast into the outer darkness in the wedding feast—after the Second Coming! Therefore, I do not feel confident in my salvation. God's grace is not enough. I need to make my "calling and election sure."*

A3 Think of the parable of the wedding banquet as a picture of salvation, not necessarily restricted to a heavenly setting after the Second Coming. Religious people of Jesus' day who rejected Him were the original audience. This is proven by the context (read Matthew 20–21 and 23). What is Jesus saying in this parable? He is saying that those He invited into His kingdom, those who were His very own (John 1:10–11), did not accept Him. Beyond that, they killed Him because they loved their religion and their religious traditions and could not accept the new wine of Jesus' teachings. Jesus insisted that He alone could give the kingdom, but that no human could ever deserve it. These people were so intent on their religion and earning God's acceptance on their own terms that they rejected Jesus, the Lamb of God who alone can give us salvation.

So, the parable tells us Jesus invited others, others who were not the Old Covenant people of God, the Gentiles. The wedding hall was filled with guests, but the person without a wedding garment was a pretender. He was there because he thought he was good enough, that what he had done and accomplished earned him a place at the wedding table. Jesus warns that no works of righteousness—being in the right place at the right time, saying and doing all of the right things, wearing the right clothes—will earn anyone entrance into the kingdom. The kingdom is given, not earned.

Your salvation, if you accept Jesus as sufficient, as enough, as being all that you can never do, is not at stake. The Holy Spirit is not a spirit of fear (2 Timothy 1:7). Jesus lives His life in those who accept Him and believe in Him (Galatians 2:20), and He is not trying to make us fail. God wants all men to be saved (1 Timothy 2:4). God has qualified us to share in the inheritance of the saints (Colossians 1:12). God is not mad at you. God is in the salvation business. That's what He does.

Of course you are lacking. I am, you are, all humans are. All that humans can ever do will never be enough. That's what grace is all about. That's what the cross of Christ and His empty tomb are all about. You will never make your calling and election sure by what you do. You will make it sure by casting yourself upon the mercies of God and accepting the riches of God's grace, believing that Jesus has done for you what you can never do. May you accept Him and rest in Him.

Q4 *I pray you will see my side this time. First Corinthians 9:24 says, "Do you not know that in a race all the runners run, but only one gets the prize? Run in such a way as to get the prize." Hebrews 12:1 says, "Therefore, since we are surrounded by such a great cloud of witnesses, let us throw off everything that hinders and the sin that so easily entangles, and let us run with perseverance the race marked out for us." In light of 2 Peter 1:1–10, we have mapped out for us the road to maturity. First, there is the act of repentance and salvation. Then we must mature as Christians in this world in which we must abide faithfully until Jesus returns. I am afraid of being chosen as a "goat" rather than a "lamb" at Judgment Day (Matthew 25:32–33). If I cannot fulfill 2 Peter 1:1–10, am I not falling short of worthiness before Christ? What if I am one of those who runs but doesn't obtain?*

A4 I see your side. I know your side. I lived in captivity to that kind of warped, twisted, legalistic, unbiblical thinking for thirty-five years. I know all about it. And, by God's grace, I reject it. I pray that in time you will as well. However, while I am attempting to help you, I also know that a man who is convinced against his will is of the same opinion still. So, yes, I see your side, but rest assured hell will

70

freeze over and the sun will fail to rise before I ever return to the prison cell of legalistic religion from which Jesus has freed me.

I have given you biblical proof that we are saved by grace. Of course we run the race that Jesus had prepared for us; of course we pick up our cross and follow Him; of course we obey. But the point is, once again, all of our efforts do not save us. We are, in fact, able to make heroic efforts because of Christ in us, the hope of glory (Colossians 1:27). We repent because repentance is a gift; we do not repent because of our inherent goodness, but because God convicts us of our sinful state. *All of it* is about God; none of it is about us. To God alone goes the glory. He has qualified us for salvation (Colossians 1:12).

We are able to abide faithfully only because Christ abides in us. If Christ is not risen, our hope is in vain. If He is risen, we have hope, for He is able to produce the fruit of the Holy Spirit within us. On our own, based upon our sinful human nature, we are not able to please God. Period. End of story. That's why the gospel of Jesus Christ is such incredibly good news!

The basis of our being a lamb rather than a goat is the Lamb of God. He alone can transform us from imperfection to His perfection, imparting His righteousness to us. We all fall short, of and by ourselves. No one is worthy, of and by themselves. All have sinned and come short of God's glory (Romans 3:23). No human can, on the basis of what they do, "make it" or "qualify." We, the undeserving, are the recipients of God's lavish, unconditional love (John 3:16).

I don't know who has told you or convinced you of something other than the gospel, but you are listening to another gospel (Galatians 1:6–10), which is, in fact, no gospel (because it's not good news) at all. What you believe is depressingly bad news, and I pray that you will yield to Jesus Christ's good news to replace the doubt, fear, and worry that are part of the performance-based religion that enslaves you.

Does God's grace mean we can get away with anything?

Q *I know that salvation is based on grace and not works, but why does the Bible have many Scriptures that urge people to do good works? What is the difference between a legalistic approach and a Christlike approach to good works? Since God wants Christians to reflect Jesus Christ, it seems that we must work hard together for that to happen. Shouldn't we maintain an emphasis on what God wants us to do? We each have to sacrifice and give of our time, talent, and resources.*

A Several things often happen when a Christian starts to place a primary focus on doing good works:

1. They become convinced that what they are doing is of far greater spiritual importance than it actually is. The focus of their spiritual lives easily slips away from what Jesus does to what they are doing.

2. They start to compare what they are doing with what others are doing, and in most cases, not doing.

3. They eventually draw lines in theological sand (lines that are not drawn by the Bible) about who is a Christian and who is not, who is a better Christian and who is inferior.

There is nothing wrong with placing an emphasis on good works, but an emphasis on good works in authentic Christianity is always the cart following the horse rather than the other way around. Jesus is the workhorse that is pulling the cart on which we ride. We do not pull Him along after us. So ^ Christians, we will do good works, but we should alv ^ God the glory, reminding ourselves and others that the "horse" power to do good works comes from Him.

The difference between a legalistic approach and an authentic Christian approach is that the Christian is always looking at Jesus, always aware of why the cart of good works is moving. I am reminded of an old story about a father who invites his son to help him mow the lawn. The son is so small that he can't even reach the handles of the lawnmower, so the father must lift him up as well as push the mower. At the end of the task, the young boy is convinced that he helped his father mow the yard, and his father praises the young man for being willing to "help" even though the little boy actually made the job much more difficult. Likewise, God condescends to use imperfect and sinful humans as His tools. But woe unto us if we get the idea that we are doing something righteous of and by our own power.

You say that "God wants Christians to reflect Jesus Christ." Well, I would put it another way. Authentic Christians will reflect Jesus. His light will shine in us because He will live His life within us. We do not produce that light. We do not even decide that we will reflect Jesus Christ. That's His decision, to use us to glorify Him.

We do choose to accept God's gift of repentance, to surrender trying to earn God's love and instead accept His grace. We decide that our pathetic attempts to shine some kind of light are just that—pathetic—and the only light worth shining is the light of Jesus. We do that by yielding our lives to Him so that He may produce His works within us, so that it is not our lives that we live, but the life of the Son of Man who loved us and gave Himself for us.

What will such an emphasis on grace lead to? First and foremost, God's grace leads us to repent of any idea that our spiritual performance has any eternal merit, to lay all our earthly, temporal trophies and crowns before Him, to surrender all, and ask Him to do for us what we cannot do for ourselves. If we do that then God will do in us what He wants to make of us. As Ephesians 2:10 says, "We are God's workmanship." That's why He saves us. He saves us not because we are good, but because He is. He saves us not because of our works, but so that He can produce His works in us. Our works are nothing; His works are everything. That's why so few people surrender, and that's why there are so many protests in Christendom that grace simply leads to permissiveness and easy-believism—the popular idea that you can be a Christian without obedience to Christ. Humans want to be in charge. We want to be in control. We want to think that what we are doing is significant and important. But in terms of our salvation, what we do has no significance. None whatsoever.

How does a pastor preach to "perfect" people?

Q *I am a pastor and have long thought that the way we Christians present our doctrines and ideas leaves much to be desired. How do I, as a pastor, handle well-meaning people who have it all wrong?*

For example, our denomination considers it important to live a holy life, not to earn salvation but out of gratitude. Many of our members have misconstrued that to mean we must be perfect like Jesus in order to "stay saved" or we can't call ourselves Christians. I've actually heard some of them say they no longer sin. Our official doctrine makes perfection a goal to be worked toward, with no expectation to reach it in this life. If we continue to aim for the target, I think we will obey God. When we willingly turn from that target and aim in another direction (willful sin), we are clearly not demonstrating our gratitude for the gift of grace.

So, in your opinion, what is the best way to combat sound doctrines that have been traditionalized to mean something else without destroying good fellowship among believers?

A Many people who go to church want to be assured that what they already believe is true. William Sloan Coffin once put it this way: "The church is full of people who are seeking that which they have already found and only want to become that which they already are." They are not receptive to a message which upsets the status quo. Therein lies the challenge and the danger of ministry.

Jesus was not received with open arms. Matthew 23 is a summary of Jesus' clash with organized and accepted religion of His day. I believe that Jesus' reception by much of religion that claims to be organized and dedicated to Him—the world of Christendom at large—would be much the same today. At the bottom line, where the rubber hits the road, people generally opt for religious ritual, tradition, deeds, programs, and beliefs rather than the grace of God.

The "best way" to confront people who are convinced that their deeds, their obedience, their quest for perfection is critically important to their salvation? Preach Jesus. Preach the gospel. All that is said and done in the context of church should be centered in Christ. Anything that threatens to take the place of Christ, or demand equal time—however innocent, pure, and true the issues may be—anything that does not focus on Jesus can and often will lead people away from authentic Christianity.

Many of us use computers every day, at work and in our homes. Computers have what is called a default, when one needs to reboot and start over again. When humans reboot, we always default, by virtue of our sinful human nature, to what we can do, how we can do it, and how much of it we need to do. We naturally default, in terms of religion, to performance. We do not automatically default to God's grace; we do not automatically see our contributions to salvation as worthless.

Many fall for the same kind of performance-based theological combination plate (think of a Mexican restaurant) that at the end of the day amounts to the same kind of religious fast food others partake of at some other church. Their church may serve chicken tacos, or cheese enchiladas, or a beef tostada, while we, at our church, are given tamales. But it's all made in the same religious kitchen; it all comes with religious rice and beans. Okay, enough of the metaphor. It's breaking down!

We humans are easy prey for anyone who tells us that our contribution to salvation is critically important. Some Christians speak of entire sanctification. Some emphasize holiness. Some, like those who adhere to the official Catholic position, see justification as primarily a human work in which we are assisted and helped by the Holy Spirit. Any of these theological "combination plates" give people the illusion of control, the illusion that what they do has a direct bearing on their salvation.

But the great hymn teaches "I surrender *all*." All. There is no way to teach God's grace without being Christ-centered. May God bless you as you minister the gospel of Jesus Christ and give you strength and courage to do so.

Once saved, always saved?

Q *Many Christians believe the "once saved, always saved" concept. What if someone was saved but then lost their love for Jesus and gradually slipped back into their old way of life? Is it possible that a person like that never experienced a genuine and sincere conversion? I know that God's grace is free and unconditional, but what is the point if all you have to do is say a little prayer, get saved, go to church a few times, and then decide you would rather live a sinful life? It would seem discouraging and unfair to those who are truly struggling to obey God. When I see people like that and am told that they're still saved no matter what, I can't help but feel resentful. Then I wonder why I'm trying so hard. I'm ashamed to feel this way. Please help me with an answer.*

A Virtually no one debates that we humans save ourselves solely by virtue of our deeds and accomplishments. The vast majority of Christians will academically agree that God saves us because we cannot save ourselves, that we are saved by grace. But, having been saved, how do we "remain" saved, how do we "maintain" our salvation? That is the question many debate.

There are two potential answers. Some say that we are saved initially by grace, but we need to do the right things often enough in order to stay saved. So their position is that salvation is a combination of what God does and what we do.

Others say that we are saved initially by grace and that we remain saved by grace. All of our salvation is by grace; all of it is about Jesus and what He has done, is doing, and will do. None of it is about us. This perspective is what I see as a bib-

and consistent position. I believe we are given
n we are saved, not conditional life based upon
ourselves from that point on.

what's the point if all we have to do is "say a little
prayer," as you say, go to church a few times, and no matter
what we do we are saved? The point is that salvation is not at
all about what we do. If it were, we would compare ourselves
with others, thinking that the things we did—the frequency,
amount, and effort we exerted—was better than that of others;
therefore, we would claim to be entitled to more.

But God's grace is not about human perceptions of entitle-
ment. It is perfectly natural to feel resentful about those
who appear to be "getting away" with something. Our sense
of human justice cries out for them to "get theirs." As children, we point out the shortcomings of others to authority
figures such as parents and teachers, hoping that they will be
penalized or punished. There is, of course, one person whose
shortcomings we do not point out to the authorities—that
would be us. We enjoy "telling on" others but seldom "tell on"
ourselves.

Read the parable in Matthew 20:1–16 with this question
in mind. Some who worked in the vineyard did not work as
long or as hard, but they received the same wage (grace). Those
who worked harder and longer were offended because they had
to stand in line and watch others receive the same gift. The
owner could have avoided the contention and controversy by
paying the people who had worked all day first and then letting them go home. But those who had worked hardest and
longest had to stand at the end of the line and watch everyone
else get the same pay (grace). When they became resentful and
protested (v. 12), the owner said, "I want to give the man who

was hired last the same as I gave you. Don't I have the right to do what I want with my own money? Or are you envious because I am so generous?" (vv. 14–15).

Is it possible that some will be saved and then become as sinful or even more so than they were before they were saved? The Bible says no. The Bible says that when we are saved, we are still in the flesh and we will still sin (1 John 1:8), but having been saved, we have now crossed from death to life (John 5:24) and Jesus now lives His resurrected life in us (Galatians 2:20). If we have been saved, we are now spiritually alive. Before that, we were spiritually dead. Dead people can't produce any good works. But those who are alive in Christ are His workmanship, "created in Christ Jesus to do good works" (Ephesians 2:10). That means that God saves us not because of what we have done or will do, but so that He can do good things in and through us. We are not saved *by* works, but *for* works. God then brings forth the fruit of the Holy Spirit in our lives (Galatians 5:22–25). This means that He will produce fruit in us because He has saved us.

Is it possible for people to be told that they are saved, to think that they are saved, and for others to think that they are saved, but they are not? First John 2:19 says that some went out from the church who never were in it. Such a thing is not only possible but also probable. Some believe regular church attendance is the acid proof of authentic Christianity. But church attendance, like any other external work, has no absolute eternal significance. Many attend church for all kinds of reasons—political, social, romantic, family, to keep parents happy, or to keep themselves from feeling guilty. They may or may not be saved.

We do not have the capability to judge who is a true Christian and who is not—and thank God we do not. If humans could determine authentic Christianity, some might feel justified in doing virtually anything to get people to repent (somewhat like the Spanish Inquisition). God alone is our judge. Salvation is by faith alone, grace alone, and Christ alone. Not much external to go by, is there?

Are the Ten Commandments still relevant?

Q *Are the Ten Commandments relevant to the modern world? Or have the Ten Commandments been completely replaced by something better?*

A Are the Ten Commandments "relevant" to our world? Yes, of course. Extremely relevant. But I suspect that you may be asking whether the Ten Commandments are required for salvation. No, they are not. Are Christians living under the requirement of the Ten Commandments (which are the core of the Old Covenant)? No. Or are we, as Christians, living under the New Covenant, based upon the Old Covenant? Yes, of course.

The complete teaching of Scripture, including the Old Testament itself, is that Christians who accept Jesus Christ as Lord and Savior are no longer under the terms of the Old Covenant.

The Ten Commandments are part of the Old Covenant. Interestingly, all of the Ten Commandments are reiterated under the New Covenant but are made more profound and meaningful. Jesus does some of this in what we call the Sermon on the Mount (Matthew 5–7). For example, He states that the commandment not to kill includes not being angry with and hating your brother or sister.

The New Testament has many lists of sins and virtues. Colossians 3 is one example; Galatians 5 is yet another. But under the New Covenant, the emphasis is on what Christ has done for us that we could never do for ourselves. The emphasis is not on the works we perform but on the righteousness Jesus produces in us. By Jesus' perfect work on the cross, He has rescued and saved us from sin. We are sinners and all need salvation. Salvation can come only one way, by grace, and only through Jesus.

We cannot earn salvation, but having been saved and rescued by the blood of Jesus Christ, we can do only one thing: obey Jesus and follow Him. Jesus made it clear that Christians no longer follow Moses and Abraham, but we follow the living Lord, who is not dead and buried, but who lives as our Advocate and High Priest. He is Savior and Lord.

After you're saved, do you need to be obedient?

Q *I believe that the Bible teaches that once we are saved, the Lord requires obedience from His children so that we can walk in His blessings, hear His voice, be in close communion with Him, and walk in power and victory. I think the Bible does say that God will bless those whose hearts are wholly committed to Him and who are walking according to His commands. We already know we don't have to live by the law since Christ is the fulfillment of it, but don't we need to obey Him?*

A You say that you "think the Bible does say that God will bless those whose hearts are wholly committed to Him and who are walking according to His commands." But exactly where does it promise such a thing to Christians, and what kind of blessings do you mean? The Old Testament promised the nation of Israel physical blessings for obedience to the Old Testament law. The New Testament promises us the spiritual blessing of eternal life not because we are obedient but because of Christ's obedience. That promise is not conditional on our behavior. Our salvation is not based on a *quid pro quo* arrangement. It is, in fact, legalistic to "think that we need to obey Him in order to hear or receive from Him."

Christians definitely do obey God. But how? Paul's answer is simple: "Live by the Spirit, and you will not gratify the desires of the sinful nature" (Galatians 5:16). Paul says that the acts of the sinful nature are obvious, and he lists the contrasting fruit of the Spirit (Galatians 5:20–23). If you belong to Christ, Paul explains, you've crucified the sinful nature and you live by the Spirit. You obey because you have been saved.

However, that simple and direct explanation falls short of what many of us want. As humans, we are more comfortable with lists of dos and don'ts. Not content with "walking in the Spirit," we seem to need some external motivation to behave correctly and to avoid the acts of the sinful nature. Paul's epistles are full of sin lists and reminders about what the Spirit-led life looks like as opposed to a life wholly given over to the sinful nature. Yet, many Christians actually seem more comfortable with a codified law, religious rules, and regulations, adding commentary to further define the law in greater detail. And as a result, many are enslaved by religion and legalism instead of enjoying the freedom of Christianity.

It's about God, not us. A narrow focus on our own obedience and our own "religion" invariably means we become discouraged, compulsive legalists. A focus on what Jesus has done and is doing for us (Hebrews 12:2) means that everything else, including our obedience, will fall into line. That's what it means to rest in Jesus.

Doesn't the Bible say we will be rewarded for our works?

Q *Are we, as Christians, supposed to work to earn rewards for heaven? Or is this just another tactic religion uses to get people to serve in churches and congregations by dangling future rewards in front of them? I long to hear God say, "Well done, my good and faithful servant," but I feel more likely to just sneak by and barely make it. Is what I do as a Christian in this life going to determine what I do in heaven? Why do we need extra rewards anyway? Are there different social classes in heaven?*

A Salvation is by grace. That message is crystal clear in the Bible. But legalism and religious manipulation have many devices and techniques that attempt to nullify, modify, and diminish the power of God's grace. One device is to say that we are saved by grace *and* works. Wrong! Another teaching is that Jesus saves us initially—He gets us started, making a "down payment" on our salvation—but from then on it's up to us. Wrong again! Still others say, in an attempt to control and manipulate, that salvation is by grace but our reward is by works. They go on to say that we can determine our "place" in heaven by what we do now. Wrong again!

But, as you say, there are biblical passages that seem to teach that there are levels of rewards in heaven. What about the parable of the talents (Matthew 25), the pounds [or minas]

(Luke 19), and the passage that speaks of how our glorified, post-resurrection bodies will have different kinds of splendor (1 Corinthians 15:35–41)? And other passages, such as 1 Corinthians 3:11–15, 2 Corinthians 5:10, and Revelation 22:12 are understood by some to teach that while we are saved by grace, we will be rewarded based on our works and performance.

Matthew 20 records the parable of the workers in the vineyard, showing that each worker received the same pay even though each worked a different number of hours. The workers did the job they were given, at the time it was offered, and all of it was accomplished by God's grace. God's grace, His gracious invitation into the work of His vineyard, enabled all of the effort to be exerted. So we are saved by grace, and salvation is the same for us all—eternity in God's presence. On the other hand, the Bible does speak of degrees of rewards. But is it accurate to say that while we are given salvation by grace, the degree of reward, or status if you like, depends on our works? Isn't that contradictory?

The answer is that our salvation and our reward are both by grace. There would be no salvation, nor would there be a reward without grace. "Levels" or "degrees" of rewards the Bible speaks of are based upon *opportunities* that are given by God's grace. God determines precisely which gifts or opportunities we are given, when we are given them, and how many we are given. In the parables of the talents and pounds/minas, the servants are given differing amounts. Catch that. The servants are *given* gifts. Yes, they either use the gifts or fail to use the gifts, but the very fact that they possess gifts speaks of God's grace.

Rewards in heaven are not based on what we produce, how well we perform, or how much we accomplish. Rather, they are based on *unique opportunities* that we are given by God's grace.

Rewards in heaven are not the result of the works-based right-eousness of performance-based religion.

Rewards in heaven happen, just as they do in our earthly lives, because some humans are given more, and more is expected, in terms of yielding oneself to God so that He may use those gifts to produce His workmanship in us (Ephesians 2:10). Jesus is the vine, we are the branches . . . we produce the fruit. We do not produce fruit because we work hard; fruit is not produced in and through us because of our diligence but because of Jesus. Yes, we are called to yield ourselves to the Master, to be living sacrifices (Romans 12:1), and to pick up our cross and follow Jesus (Luke 9:23). Grace means that we will be active in God's service. But we should never get the idea that what we are doing is going to save us, or that what we are doing is going to cause us to be better or superior to others, either on this side or the other side of eternity.

There are those who hold out the biblical teaching of rewards like some carrot (or, as you say, by "dangling future rewards") to motivate and, sadly, to manipulate (2 Peter 2:3). Religious legalism twists and distorts biblical teaching about rewards to control its followers, but its take on heavenly rewards is not Christ-centered, nor is it based on God's amazing grace.

WHY DOES GOD
ALLOW SUFFERING?

*God is doing nothing to protect
innocent children!*

Q *Where is God when poor, little, innocent children are abducted, raped, and killed? I'm so tired of it all. Every week, another beautiful little child is being killed or scarred for life by one of these perverts. I don't even know why I keep taking my two small kids to Sunday school and telling them to pray and that God will be there for them, because He won't. The hate in this rotten world is just too much. Why keep praying for these children to be safe when it is obviously a waste of time?*

I don't blame God, if there even is one, for ignoring me, because I have sinned many times in my life and done some rotten things. But for God to do nothing to protect these wonderful, happy children from perverts—well, it's just too much.

A In many ways, your question is echoed by people everywhere, those who believe in God and those who do not. Some blame God for horrible and tragic situations like you describe, but their supposition is wrong. God never told us that He would only allow certain kinds of sin, but not others.

God has made us all creatures of choice. He allows choice, and those choices run from Genghis Khan, Adolph Hitler, and Saddam Hussein to serial killers and rapists, as well as the kinds made by petty thieves and corporate embezzlers. He has allowed little children to be molested by men who wore priestly vestments. God allows cheating on income taxes, drug abuse, drunk drivers, and adultery. He allows obese people to eat themselves into an early grave and people to smoke themselves into having cancer. He doesn't stop any of it.

How can He stop such behaviors if His plan involves free choice for His children? There is an alternative: He could have created humans as robots with certain behaviors preprogrammed. We would always be kind and considerate to all humans, even our own family (sometimes the hardest people for humans to love are those to whom we are closest!). We would never take any illicit drugs; we would always be faithful to our spouses. Our language would always be without profanity. We would always do exactly what we were preprogrammed to do.

However, God didn't do things that way. Another possibility: God could have decided not to share the universe with His human children at all because, after all, with humans there is always one big mess after another. Why on earth, when Jesus founded His church, did He decide to allow humans to be a part of it? Why not just angels? From the moment church membership in the universal body of Christ was available to human beings, big problems were inevitable. And the church has had its scandals, from inquisitions and crusades to ministers running away with the church treasury and pastors running away with the church secretaries, loving money and their lusts more than the sheep of God's flock. Why did God do it the way He did?

We really don't know why God allows bad things to happen, do we? God hasn't told us, but one thing is for sure: the fact that God allows suffering, combined with the fact that we humans are often horrified by human behavior, doesn't mean that God doesn't exist or that He doesn't care or love us.

We remember at least two things in all of this:

1. We are all sinners. Our sin is different from others, in matters of degrees, but sin is sin. We all fall short. We need the cross of Christ to save us from the death penalty of our sin (Romans 6:23). We need this supreme act of love from God in the flesh. As Paul tells us in Romans, we remember that God didn't die for us because we had been such good little girls and boys. He didn't wait to die for us until He had assurances that we would respond in kind, and because of His sacrificial love we would always be on our best behavior. He loved us, and still does, because He is holy, just, and pure, because He is righteous and perfect, not because of how good we are. God loves us, all of us, even the most rotten of us, and offers all of us the same forgiveness, the same reconciliation. The blood of Christ is for us all. We must reach out to Him and accept it. That is something many of us find nearly impossible to do, for we must repent of who and what we are and accept the reality that we, of and by ourselves, have done nothing but screw up our own lives and the lives of many others. For that reason, many do not receive and accept the free gift of God.

2. We remember that Jesus rose from the dead in victory, and that His resurrection means He is still here with us now. We may ask Him to live His life in us, and He will. The life that we can live is not the way we used to live, not the sinful life of this flesh, but the life of our risen Lord (Galatians 2:20). Through Jesus we can have victory over the sin and corruption

that is part of what it means to live in this flesh, and to have eternal life, the free gift of God, by His grace. We may have the assurance that there will come a day when we will rise from the dead and we will have new bodies, resurrection bodies, like that of Jesus (see 1 Corinthians 15 and 1 John 3:1–3). We will live with God forever, in incorruptible, immortal bodies that are free of this sinful flesh. That is our hope! The resurrection is our hope, our victory, given to us by God's grace.

What about all those who do not accept God's grace? God doesn't tell us how and when He will work in their lives. In one sense, exactly what He does and when He does what He does or does not do is not our problem. We do have a problem, though—us. We can't do much to change other people, can we? We all have the power of choice. We can't take that away from others, for it is God-given. What can we do? We can change ourselves—that's where it all starts. Let's start accepting Jesus at His word in our lives. Let's start yielding to the new life in Christ in our lives. Let's repent of our sins. Let's be who and what God wants us to be. Let's reflect the light and love of Christ Jesus in our lives. It's easy to blame God. It's easy to blame others. It's so comforting and selfishly reassuring because such blaming makes us feel less responsible. But in fact we are responsible. Let's do what we can do now, and then through Christ living in us, through allowing Him to use us as His tools, perhaps others may see the love of God.

Does God care?

Q *Is God active in our world? We have major disasters. Does God simply watch horrible catastrophes take place without doing anything? Doesn't He care? Sometimes my existence seems to be a big joke. What is there to hope for when everything is bad and you can do nothing about it?*

A God has a plan and He is active in the world, but "active" by His definition, not ours. Some people think God must not exist, or if He does, He doesn't care because He allows disasters and accidents to happen. But God never told us in the Bible that such things would not happen; in fact, He said that they would, to those who are believers as well as those who are not. The rain falls on the just and the unjust (Matthew 5:45). In His day, Jesus used the example of a tower that had fallen in Siloam (Luke 13:4) to explain that accidents happen. Time and chance are part of this human life that we all lead, and God has designed our lives that way. Jesus said that those who followed Him would have to take up their cross, their lives which often include sadness, sorrow, and disasters, and follow Him (Mark 8:34).

There are some who present Christianity as a life of physical abundance of health and wealth, of success and prosperity. But the Bible does not guarantee that our lives in this flesh will be one continuous walk in some idyllic park. God's plan for us is not centered on the here and now. This life is not all there is. There is more to life than what we see and understand and experience. God's plan is for eternity, the eternal spiritual reality that He offers to us all (John 3:16).

In this life, we experience pain and suffering. Jesus said, "In this world you will have trouble" (John 16:33), but in this same verse He said, "Take heart! I have overcome the world." God, in the person of Jesus, came to us and lived as one of us, being born of the virgin Mary. Jesus was God in the flesh. He humbled Himself and experienced all that we do, including suffering, heartache, betrayal, and pain to save us. Jesus' death on the cross was not to save us from this physical world, but to save us that we might enjoy eternity with Him.

We humans need God; we are not independent of Him. We do not have eternal life. We do not decide or control how long we will live, whether we will be involved in an accident, or whether we will be the victims of a virus or a disease. We need God. God is sovereign over nature, not humans.

We humans like to think that we are so advanced that we do not need God. But the fact is that without Him our life is futile and hopeless. We have no hope beyond the grave without God. But because of God, because He loves us (John 3:16) and because of Jesus Christ, who died that we might live, we have hope, both now and forever. This is the central teaching of the gospel and why the word *gospel* means "good news"! None of us needs to despair. Jesus Christ is the answer for the empty and meaningless lives that we experience apart from God.

EVANGELISM

Are Christians commanded to "win souls for Christ"?

Q *I am continually told that Christians are commanded and obligated to spread God's Word to the corners of the earth and lead people to salvation through personal witnessing. Some actually teach that personal witnessing is the defining mark of a Christian. Is personal witnessing a commanded part of being a Christian? Soul-winning advocates even preach we are, in a way, responsible for friends/family burning in hell if we don't witness, a sobering thought.*

A There is a great debate on the topic you raise. Many evangelical Christians believe (evidenced by their very name) that one of the primary duties of Christians is to personally evangelize. Aspects of this belief can be shown to be biblical in terms of sharing our faith with others. Of course, there are many ways to proclaim the gospel and share our faith that do not involve personal witnessing. I do not believe the absolute necessity of personal witnessing and "sharing our testimony" as a regular and necessary practice of our day-to-day lives can be shown from the Bible.

There are many Christians who do not feel equipped,

gifted, or talented enough to talk to strangers about Jesus as they sit next to them on a bus, on a plane, or at a bus stop. Allowing for the fact that we are all reluctant to do something that is uncomfortable but perhaps, nevertheless, something we ought to do, I still believe, based upon the gospel of Jesus Christ, that not every Christian needs to engage in this kind of personal, direct, and even, as some call it, confrontational evangelism. Trouble often arises when those who believe fervently in such a practice hear someone like me say that it is not a priority. To add more fuel to that fire, I believe this practice/expectation is yet another way that religion can worm its way into authentic Christianity.

I believe that if I happen to become involved in a conversation about God while I am on an airplane, and if both the other person and I are interested and welcome such a conversation, that such a conversation is a good thing. But if either of us is tired, or if we would prefer to read, or even if we want to watch the in-flight movie, God will still be happy with us! I don't presume to think that if I don't have a discussion with a person in row 33, seat F, that they may be lost for eternity. I don't presume that I am the only way that God might reach that person—or anyone else for that matter.

I believe that God allows me to be of use in His service, but He does not completely depend on how well I tell others about Him. Nor, for that matter, does the eternal fate of others depend on how effectively and fervently I evangelize. The very idea smacks of works, righteousness, and performance-based, legalistic religion rather than God's amazing grace. Some churches, groups, and theological constructs would have me believe that another person's eternity is largely up to me. If they can persuade me of such a belief, then I am going to be continually, perhaps to the point of making myself into a pest to others, telling people about my denominational brand of Jesus and also inviting them to my religious club, which is of course better than any other religious club. It seems to me that one of the transparent religious motives of such a practice is the growth of a group, church, or congregation—for if we tell others, our friends, family, etc., if we convince them and persuade them, our church or group will grow.

Is it wrong for a church to grow? Not at all. But is any method used for growth justified? And what's the motive for church growth? Can a healthy church not grow? Yes, there are many reasons why a healthy church may not grow. Generally, Christianity grows and churches grow, but the desire to build and grow legally incorporated religious entities is not the primary reason for which God has placed us here on earth. Can unhealthy churches, can cults grow? Of course they can. Can cults have effective evangelistic techniques? Of course they can, and they do. Is the number of converts that we individually or corporately make directly connected to the gospel, salvation by grace? Of course not.

Christ-centered evangelism should tell others about the personal relationship we can have with Jesus, whether they join our church or not. Whether they decide to march in lockstep with all of our particular practices or not, we need to tell them about Jesus. Evangelism sometimes gets those two subjects turned around. Christ-centered evangelism is all about sharing the good news of God's amazing grace with others. But sometimes Christ-centered evangelism doesn't seem to be a good enough or an effective-enough sales point, so some evangelism gets into fear, using illogical straw men and bait-and-switch tactics, giving the general idea that if folks come to our church they will be better off than where they are. But that assumption is not necessarily biblical (see, for example, Matthew 23:15).

The mark and sign of authentic Christianity is not our salesmanship, it isn't our evangelistic tactics, and it isn't how big our church becomes; the mark of a Christian is our love (John 13:34–35). How much of the context of evangelistic methodology is based on God's love? I do not accept the idea that I will be, nor will anyone else be, responsible for someone burning in hell. I find the idea to be primitive and superstitious, an absolutely unwarranted misrepresentation of the God of the Bible. Witnessing can become manipulative, a technique religion can use to control its followers. Our evangelism needs to be Christ-centered—it's not about how much success we find; it's about telling others about Him, whether they join our church or denomination or not.

Do I reject evangelism? Not at all. I believe that we should tell others about Jesus. But I don't believe in evangelism at any price. I don't believe that the end justifies the means. I don't believe in placing unbiblical burdens on people in the name of church growth. I don't believe in fear religion. I believe in telling people about God. I believe that God, in His mercy and grace, in His providence, in His time, according to His perfect and holy will, decides how and when to use us as His tools, and when He may use some other way or some other time to speak to those He issues an invitation. I believe that we are all, as Christians, a living sacrifice, and that we live a life of service in the name of our Savior. We all have been given differing gifts and abilities, and we should yield to our Lord and Savior (which isn't always the same as religion!) so that He might use us as He wishes.

Must Christians "witness"?

Q *What is our role once we believe and accept Jesus Christ and live according to the Bible? Is it then our responsibility to bring the Christian way of life to neighbors, friends, and family? Can a believer just live a quiet life, minding his or her own business? I've always been taught that Christians have an obligation to go out and "witness" to the unchurched. Can you explain this more clearly?*

A The New Testament tells us a great deal about the Christian role—to be salt and light, to shine the light of Christ (or perhaps more correctly, to reflect the light that He lives within us) so that others can see and perhaps come to know Jesus through us. But how this happens is not specifically made known or revealed. How persistent we should be, how confrontational we should be—that is not specified in the Bible.

Some denominations suggest that members need to witness to unbelievers virtually every day—on the bus, on the train, at the grocery store, etc. Some churches essentially believe that if you are not one of their members, you need a "witness." This teaching implies there is a quota that members of such churches must meet. Other churches and denominations (the majority of Christian churches, in fact) do not suggest such a thing— saying that the Christian role is less active and more passive in terms of allowing our lives and deeds to be evident, but like a light we need not make noise or be confrontational in order to be a tool in God's hands.

There are many who need to accept the loving relationship God offers them, but given the hard sell to which they have been subjected they will need to get over the damage done by the confrontational approach before they are ready to seek God. The confrontational approach of evangelism has done just as much harm as it may have done good. Our role in evangelism is to be more discreet, more friendly, more warm and engaging rather than the "Do you know the Lord?" routine that some "use" on complete strangers. I favor relational evangelism—tactfully talking about God and His amazing grace with those we know and with whom we enjoy a relationship—rather than the confrontational approach, which can also include appeals of fear ("get right or get left") to many who are virtual strangers.

Is there one right way to "witness"?

Q *I recently saw a new reality show on one of the major Christian television networks where people on the street are taped while being "witnessed" to. The hosts of the show follow a formula. They confront people with the Ten Commandments. If their subjects admit that they have not obeyed the Ten Commandments, then the hosts share the gospel with them. The hosts teach that this is the way the gospel ought to be shared and claim this is the way Jesus did it. Must people be confronted with the law before they are presented with the gospel? Must we "witness" to others as a part of being a Christian?*

A What you describe seems to be a mild form of confrontational evangelism. This confrontational approach is a reaction to two things: 1) easy-believism—the popular idea that you can be a Christian without obedience to Christ, and 2) postmodernism and moral relativism—the idea that there is no right or wrong or that right and wrong are subjective.

Many Christians believe they must "witness" to every unsaved person they encounter. They assume that they are personally carrying the burden of bringing this person to Christ and that if they don't make an attempt to do so, God will hold them responsible. They have been taught to infer these marching orders from passages such as Mark 16:15: "Go into all the world and preach the good news to all creation." But this instruction is given collectively to the church, not necessarily every individual believer. Further, in John 6:44, Jesus tells us, "No one can come to me unless the Father who sent me draws him, and I will raise him up at the last day." The act of conversion does not depend entirely on what we do; it depends on what God does. He may occasionally use us as His instruments in that process, but God is the only one who can truly bring a human being to repentance and salvation.

Fear is an effective evangelistic technique to get people to come to church, but at what cost? While many may have become church members to avoid hell, considering human nature and considering the number of preachers and street-corner evangelists who have ladled out hellfire and brimstone messages over the years, we must ask: is herding people into the Kingdom with the cattle prod of fear and the motive of self-preservation really what God prefers? People may become a member of a church because of being motivated by fear, but is that necessarily the same as genuine conversion?

Second to our relationship with God, our relationships with other human beings are the most important thing and the most effective catalyst in reaching people for Christ. St. Francis of Assisi put it well: "In everything preach the gospel—if necessary, use words." We limit our effectiveness and fail to adequately reflect God's love for others when we reduce sharing the good news to a formula. Instead of real relationships and friendships, we may come to see people as objects to be acquired for our group, sales to be closed, or foes to be vanquished. Some "win a soul" for Jesus and put another notch in the handle of their spiritual six-shooter. Jesus was not motivated by a sense of duty or witnessing quotas, but by His infinite love and concern for each individual He encountered. As He lives in us, may we share that love with others.

What happens to the unsaved when they die?

Q I have a question about what happens to the unsaved when they die. Are they going to die and be forgotten forever? Or will they forever be separated from God and their saved loved ones? I have a sister who died thirteen years ago at the age of twenty-one. I don't know if she ever accepted Jesus as her Savior, and I am very concerned for her soul.

A The Bible does not offer an exact and precise description of what will happen to those who have died having never accepted Christ. It is true that some churches, and religion in general, often attempt to "scare us into heaven" by holding our feet over the burning hot coals of hell. But such manipulation is not the way God reaches out to us. God assures us that He loves us all, that He gave His Son that we should not perish, and that Jesus did not come to condemn the world (John 3:16–17).

The Bible does not give any human the discernment that we need to determine who is saved or who has been saved. It notes that such judgments belong to God alone. Therefore, while it may seem to us that some might not have been saved, we cannot humanly always make such a dogmatic determination. God graciously allows us to be of help and assistance in telling others about the gospel, but He never indicates that our efforts alone (nor that of organized entities) will determine whether someone is saved or not. How God saves and when He does is not completely revealed to us. In addition, God assures us that "eye hath not seen" the wonderful things that He has prepared for us (1 Corinthians 2:9 KJV). We cannot imagine the wonderful things God has in store; He will reveal them in eternity future.

As much as you are concerned for your sister's soul, you may be assured that God is far more concerned and that He loves each of His children equally. However manifestly unfair things might seem to be, whatever our limited perspective may be, at the end of the day our perspective is just that—limited. Your sister is in God's loving embrace. Be assured of His love for you and for her.

GOD

How can God "sit" on the right side of Himself?

Q *How can Jesus, the Son of God, sit on the right side of the Father and still be God (Romans 8:34; Colossians 3:1)? How can God sit on the right side of Himself?*

A The Bible speaks of God in human language, using human reality and mortality to describe heavenly eternity. When the Bible says that God is "in" heaven, it does not mean that God is confined to any place, nor does it mean that heaven is a "place." Heaven is a state of existence that is outside time and space, but in order to think about it and talk about it, humans have to speak of being "there." The Bible tells us that God is omnipresent—everywhere at once. He does not need to travel to be somewhere where He is now not present, nor does He vacate a "place" to be somewhere else.

When the Bible speaks of God having arms, hands, and features of human anatomy, it is using anthropomorphic language (using human language to attribute human characteristics to a non-human). God, who inspired the Bible, is using terminology we understand in order to reveal Himself to us. In doing so, He has to condescend to our level for we are unable to rise to His level of understanding. It is somewhat like an adult parent talking to a child using silly, childish language, using the sounds of an animal ("moo" for a cow) or a vehicle ("choo-choo" for a train) to describe reality beyond a child's comprehension.

Thus, it is illogical to think that God cannot be one, yet three co-equal and co-essential divine Persons because we conclude that He cannot sit on the right side of Himself. The term "sitting" and sitting in any "place" as geographically or directionally defined (by human limitations of time and space) are not literal descriptions when used to speak of God. Physical boundaries, such as right or left, north or south, are terms which are not precise or accurate to use of the one, true God. They are used by Him to help us—His children whom He loves with a perfect love—to understand Him. We cannot fully comprehend His totality because we are not created by Him with the capacity to do so. In His mercy, God has, in the Person of Jesus, become one of us so that we might become one with Him.

Why did Jesus have to suffer?

Q Why did Jesus have to suffer such excruciating pain before His death? If it just takes His blood to pay for our sins, why wasn't a quick death enough?

A While Jesus was God in the flesh and His divinity meant that His life was worth all of ours and could therefore pay for all of our sins, He was also human. In His humanity, He experienced the pain and suffering that we do or can in our earthly lives. The fact that Jesus suffered, bled, and died for us makes God seem more intimate and real to us. Christians have a God who is a part of His creation, who became one of us, and who was willing to experience our hurts and pains. He didn't declare Himself exempt from our experience, quickly and clinically doing only what needed to be done.

How does the death of Jesus pay for our sins?

Q *The Bible states that the wages of sin is death and that Jesus paid for this debt by dying on the cross. How could the death of one person pay for the sin of all humanity?*

A Jesus was not simply another man who somehow was able to live a sin-free life, for if that were the case then He would have been able only to "buy" His own eternal life with His perfection.

The Bible teaches that God came to us in the Person of Jesus, becoming a human while remaining divine. He became something He had not been before (human) while not ceasing to be God.

Because He was the God-man, His life and death are worth more than the sum total of all men and women who have ever lived and who ever will. The Creator died for His creation. The Creator, perfect, superior, and greater than what is formed and created, voluntarily became one with His imperfect and inferior creation to save it from sin. The debt is paid.

Does the Trinity matter?

Q *I honestly don't know whether God is triune or not; I don't see it taught in Scripture. However, I believe in God the Father, in the Lord Jesus Christ His beloved Son, my Savior, and in the Holy Spirit of God. I don't see that it matters* *whether I believe in something just because it is a tradition. If one has to believe a doctrinal statement to be a true Christian, then grace is diminished. God's gift of salvation is entirely free, dependent only on God's choice. You cannot attach conditions or it no longer is of grace—rather, it is of works.*

A Simply believing in a tradition does not make one a true Christian. I believe that the only Something that one must accept in order to be a Christian is Jesus Christ, but that belief is absolutely unconditional, without reservation. It is not Jesus *plus* things we need to do, believe, recite, or memorize. It is Jesus alone.

I believe that there are cognitive, theological, and biblical conclusions that most Christians will eventually accept once they believe in Jesus alone through faith and grace alone. One of those conclusions is the Trinity. You say you believe in the Father, Son, and Holy Spirit. *How* are they Father, Son, and Holy Spirit?

There are Christians who have not been taught about the nature of God. In spite of their lack of academic awareness of God's triune nature, I believe that they are Christians by God's grace. No essay test about the nature of God is administered outside of the gates of God's kingdom of heaven, nor are we denied entrance until we achieve a high-enough score. God does not keep the gates of heaven locked until we repeat, word for word, the words of the Nicene or Apostles' Creed.

There are no conditions to grace. We are saved by grace alone. Period. Having said that, we must *not* then conclude that everyone who says, "Lord, Lord" will be saved either (Matthew 7:21). By studying the history of the Christian faith, we can see the central attributes of authentic Christianity over the centuries. There are hallmarks of the workmanship that God has called us to (Ephesians 2:10)—the fruit that He produces in the lives of Christians.

Belief in some formulation of one God, who is Father, Son, and Holy Spirit, has always been a central issue within historic Christianity. To state the opposite, there is one constant that is *always* present in cultic teaching, the denial of the God of the Bible as one God who is three in Person. So what can we conclude? Those who receive God's grace and who accept Jesus Christ as Lord and Savior are eventually given insight and understanding about the nature of God. God reveals Himself to us, perhaps in slightly differing ways but never in conflicting ways. Some Christians have a little better comprehension of God, some a little less. Our intellectual comprehension of God is not what saves us, nor is it the sole basis of knowing Him intimately. God, who is Father, Son, and Holy Spirit, is the same yesterday, today, and forever, and He always reveals Himself as He is.

Are God's choices limited by His knowledge of the future?

Q *I have a logical dilemma. If God has absolute and infallible knowledge of the future, then God must have known throughout eternity everything He would ever do. Doesn't this make God a slave to His own foreknowledge and therefore powerless to act differently? Can this be consistent with a being who is all-powerful? Some Christians tell me that it's true that God must act consistently with His foreknowledge, but that it was God who in the beginning freely determined what His future actions would be. But wait a minute! If God has always existed, how could there be a "beginning," and if God is truly all-knowing, how could there be a time at which He didn't foreknow everything, including His* *own actions? How can God be all-powerful if there was never a time in all of eternity when He could freely create or decide anything? Does this mean God doesn't actually exist?*

A The logical dilemma you propose is only a dilemma if God is exactly like us. But the Bible claims otherwise, and in fact logic itself would propose that something greater must bring into existence that which is made or created. Since we exist and we can think, plan, imagine, dream, and create, then is it not logical to assume that Someone/Something greater than ourselves brought us into existence?

God knows all, He is all-knowing, whatever that means to the human mind (and there is a point at which we cannot humanly conceive of knowing "all"). God knows what He will do and always has, but we must not make the mistake of assuming the human options we have are similar to the "options" God has.

God does not necessarily need to think, react, or plan as we do. God dwells in eternity past, eternity present, and eternity future. He is not limited by our dimensions of time and space. He is not limited to human definitions and logic that attempt to put Him into a finite "box" so that we can capture and understand Him. He is bigger than our world, beyond our minds, and His nature transcends our logic. He is logical, but He is not confined to the limits of human reason. God reminds us in Psalm 50:21 that He is not "altogether like [us]." In Isaiah 55:8–9, He tells us that His thoughts are not like ours—they transcend ours "as the heavens are higher than the earth."

Because we, as humans, might not logically comprehend God, our lack of insight is not a verdict that God does not exist any more than a cow grazing in a field, unable to comprehend a jet airliner flying overhead, disproves the existence of aviation.

TATTOOS

Do tattoos honor God?

Q *A sermon in our church regarding tattoos has stirred a debate in our home, and I need your help to clarify a couple of things.*

1. Based on Leviticus 19:28 and 1 Corinthians 6:19–20, would someone who gets a tattoo be honoring God with his/her body?

2. If so, how does this differ from ear piercing?

3. How can we apply one law from the Old Testament and discard others, specifically the laws in Leviticus about cutting hair on the sides, mixing crops in the field, etc.?

A The New Covenant is not composed of 50 percent of the Old Covenant. It's not 60-40, 80-20, or even 95-5. It is all new. All of it. We cannot decide which Old Covenant laws, prohibitions, statutes, or ordinances are "in effect" and which have been nailed to the cross. No human being can do that—no minister, no priest, no scholar—for it is clear that nothing in the Old Covenant is binding/required for the Christian today. Nothing, as stipulated in the Old Covenant, is required for Christians.

There are laws and principles in the Old Covenant that teachings of the New Covenant are based upon, but when they are, they are clearly enunciated in the New Testament. If they are not, then there is no clear mandate that Christians have to pick and choose from the Old Covenant, or to teach that some of the Old Covenant is required for Christians while other parts are not.

What about your specific question . . . ear piercing, cutting hair, mixing crops, and tattoos? Sincere and well-intentioned Christians, church leaders, and pastors often decide that they need to make a statement and draw a line in the sand about what they believe to be a negative social or cultural trend. They realize that they should base their convictions in and on the Bible, so they do. They often search for and find a place in the Bible that agrees with their *a priori* conclusion. This practice is called proof-texting—or script-torture.

Years ago, when the Beatles first became popular, some Christians were convinced that their music was at the very best bad, and at the worst evil, because the Beatles had "long hair." They thus condemned the Beatles and their music by saying that long hair is a shame to a man, quoting 1 Corinthians 11:14. But, 1) that is not what the passage in 1 Corinthians means, and 2) even if it did, there are many cultural difficulties with determining what constitutes long hair for a man. For example, Roman men, at the time of the writing of 1 Corinthians, wore their hair much shorter than did the Jews of Palestine. The Beatles, and their music, may have been good, bad, or somewhere in between, but to try to force the Bible to line up behind cultural values we prefer is biblically dishonest.

Regarding tattoos: the prohibition you note in Leviticus has to do with a specific practice in that day and age that had religious overtones, not the practice that most men and women (specifically the young) find appealing today. We should not try to infer that the Bible (and hence God) agrees with us, when in fact the Bible is silent.

I personally happen to believe that a young man or woman who gets multiple tattoos is one day going to wish he or she had not covered their body with these markings. Scarring your skin with the name of a boy- or girlfriend who may well not wind up as your spouse is not a smart, long-term decision; but for those who only live in the moment, it seems exciting. Perhaps the concern of a message, a sermon, or a discussion on this topic ought to be about long-term consequences of decisions that we make today—and how we all, young and old, need to keep that principle (which is biblical) in mind.

THE MORALITY
OF WAR

Should Christians support war?

Q *Do Christians support military action? If so, why? If not, why not?*

A There are at least four biblical positions about Christians and warfare. Most countries that have some basis in the Judeo-Christian heritage allow for Christians to practice one of these four valid positions.

The first position is nonresistance. Christians who have such a position often believe that Christian participation in war should be limited to noncombatants—medics, cooks, clerical workers, etc.

A second view is pacifism. This is the most "extreme" view, in that Christians who have such a belief will not participate in war or violence in any way. Christians who are pacifists may be morally opposed to gun ownership, and they will refuse to work as security guards or as part of a police force. They believe that peace is their calling.

A third perspective is called the just-war perspective. Just war sees warfare as permissible if the warfare is defensive—in a similar way as personal safety. No Christian should offensively assault anyone else according to this view, but should Christians find themselves being physically threatened, they may defensively protect themselves and/or their loved ones and fellow citizens. Some, of course, believe that their nation follows this principle. They believe that the military of their country never offensively attacks others but only defends what is rightfully theirs or even, in some cases, some other country whose freedoms are threatened.

The fourth Christian viewpoint about war—Christians may go to war not only to defend themselves, but they may, indeed must, in the cause of justice. When outrageous and evil behavior occurs, such as that of Adolph Hitler or the al-Qaeda terrorists, then, goes this view, Christians are duty bound and obligated to stand against a moral evil. They are, given this view, agents of God standing against evil oppression (see Romans 13).

SALVATION

Exactly when does a Christian become saved?

Q *Does the Bible say anything about a specific point in time, a split-second moment when one is saved? I heard a preacher ask someone, "When did you get saved?" It took me a period of time to believe. Believing is more than accepting; it's more like trusting. And it took awhile for me to trust Jesus as my righteousness, not a split second that I can recall. I know I'm saved because of Jesus and not by anything I can accomplish on my own. What do you think? Do you think pinpointing a time and place—relying on an "experience"—can take the focus off of Christ for salvation?*

A Those who insist that everyone experience the exact kind of conversion experience they did or that everyone fit neatly into their well-ordered religious world of dos, don'ts, and dogmas are actually proclaiming their brand of religion. This kind of message would be better understood as another religious "we're better than they are because of things we do and don't do" denominationalism rather than the gospel of Jesus Christ.

Of course, conversion takes place over a period of time, and it often does not include some emotionally explosive, memorable moment in time. It can include a road-to-Damascus experience

(Acts 9), but not necessarily. A road-to-Damascus experience is not normative or required for Christians. Conversion is both an act and a process, and the process is, according to the Bible, one of the works of the Holy Spirit.

One of the best responses to the idea that everyone must have a "testimony" about the time and manner in which they "got saved" (an exercise that can quickly become legalistic spiritual one-upmanship) is an anecdote about a biblical scholar who was once asked when he was saved. He replied, "Why, I should think that was almost two thousand years ago at the cross of Christ."

May we all realize much more deeply that the cross of Christ is sufficient, and that His death on the cross and His victorious resurrection saves us. That is when we were saved.

Eternal suffering for the unsaved?

Q *I have been studying the Bible on the topic of dying in your sins, eternal condemnation, and God's judgment of mankind. This is not a pleasant topic for me, but I want to understand it. My question concerns the multitudes of humans throughout history who, it seems, will never receive salvation in their physical lifetimes. Will they die "in their sins," condemned, or is Christ's mercy extended beyond their physical life? Will they all face eternal suffering? Can you help me understand?*

A The topic you are studying is indeed unpleasant. It is troubling, especially since God does not provide dogmatic answers to all of these specific questions. Religion does, but in so doing it exceeds its authority. What will happen to those who seem to never have received salvation before they die? We don't know. God doesn't reveal specifics. We do know that "no eye has seen, no ear has heard, no mind has conceived what God has prepared for those who love him" (1 Corinthians 2:9). It is true that the Holy Spirit, as the passage continues, has revealed much to us, but there is much that remains a mystery to us. That includes the question you raise.

Many churches, in the name of God, have, in my opinion, overstepped their bounds in providing specifics about hell and eternal torment. Many Christians and churches feel, and have felt, justified in holding sinners' feet over the fiery coals of hell.

How do we know that all those who seem to have died without Christ have done so? Perhaps some or many of them have—but again, simply because a representative from our denomination did not reach some people group in Africa, India, or China does not mean that those people are doomed. This topic has been, and is being, used as leverage and motivation for Christians to support missionaries and evangelism. Of course we should tell others about the kingdom of God. But nowhere in the Bible does God tell us that the salvation of others hinges entirely on our efforts. Thank God for that! He uses us as His tools, but we are not the only tool in His toolbox! This is not, on the other hand, to minimize our efforts. It's simply to place what we do and what God will and can do in proper perspective. But God must have other ways of saving people other than our human efforts.

How many people does God reach in the last few days or hours of their lives? We don't know. How long did it take for the thief on the cross to be saved (Luke 23:40–43)? Apparently not very long. Do churches and individual Christians in general like the idea of "death-bed confessions"? No, because it means that those who do not have perfect attendance in church and those who do not give generously to the church still might have a chance to be saved at the end of their lives. Humanly, we don't like the idea of someone else getting away with something or someone not having to work as hard as we did. But Jesus asks us, "Are you envious because I am generous?" (Matthew 20:15).

Will God minister to some after they have died? We don't know. We certainly would not want to say, categorically and dogmatically, that He will, for He does not tell us such a thing. Suppose we do say that God will minister to others at some point after death and in so doing we encourage some *not* to come to Christ, leading them to think that there will be some point after they die when they can do so. Obviously, we would be in error, misleading others, and perhaps encouraging them to continue in their sins.

At the end of the day, we don't know a great deal about this topic, one way or another. And since we don't, there is cause for caution about misrepresenting God. Again, whatever He will do and whatever He is now doing that He may not have revealed to us is out of and because of His love. We do not worship a vindictive God.

Must I "work out" my own salvation?

Q If our focus ought to be on God's grace, expecting works to follow automatically from a life transformed by grace, what does the Bible mean when it tells us to "work out" our salvation? Are we not expected to perfect the salvation we have received and grow to be more and more like Him?

A It's the ever-present question—if grace really is too good to be true, then won't Christians just become slackers, goofing their way into God's kingdom of heaven, expecting God to do everything for them?

The major problem with this line of questioning is that it comes from our human experience/expectation/perspective. From our perspective, we understand cause and effect. We understand the basic bartering system. You give someone something, you do something for someone, and in return they respond. That's the way humans work. But that's not the way God works. We cannot mow God's lawn and then expect Him to pay us. We cannot rake the leaves in His backyard, we can't dust or clean heaven, and we can't make Him a wonderful dinner. When we read and understand God's revelation, the gospel of Jesus Christ, we know that our relationship with God is not based on human interactions. But we think, given the way our world works, that if we do things for Him then He will be happier with us than He would have otherwise been.

On the one hand, God is happier with us if we do our best not to lie, not to steal, and not to gossip. However, doing and not doing things does not earn us credit or demerits with God. That's where our reasoning often leaves the track, and we wind up locked into a performance-based relationship with God.

God's relationship with us is not conditional. He loves us because He is good, not because or when we are good. Given that eternal reality, given the gospel of Jesus Christ, given the fact that God loves us in spite of who we are, we must understand that while we should try to be good, all of our doing does not alter or modify our relationship with God. Further, it is helpful to realize that the power and often the motivation to do the right thing comes from Jesus Christ, who lives His life within us.

Should we do good things? Of course. Should we exhort

and encourage one another to do the right things? Yes. Should we browbeat and threaten one another about the consequences of not doing the right things? Should we imply that doing right things gains us some standing with God that we would have not otherwise enjoyed? No. Do many in Christendom promise that our reward, our standing with God and God's opinion of us will increase if we do more of the right things? Yes. Should they, according to the gospel? No.

Jesus is both our Savior and our Lord. That means He saves us, giving us eternal life, by God's grace, and because of His cross. He freely gives us eternal life that we can never earn. It means that He is our Lord, that because He has saved us we obey Him, we follow Him, and we dedicate our lives to Him. Christians are, by definition, obedient people. We are obedient to Jesus Christ because we have been saved. Christians are not obedient so that they can become saved; they are obedient because they have been. Obedience is a consequence of salvation. It is not a causal agent of salvation.

What does it mean to "work out" your salvation? I believe you have Philippians 2:12 in mind. Here's what it says: "Therefore, my dear friends, as you have always obeyed—not only in my presence, but now much more in my absence—continue to work out your salvation with fear and trembling." That's the end of verse 12, but the sentence does not end. Verse 12 ends with a comma and the sentence continues in verse 13. And what does verse 13 say? "For it is God who works in you to will and to act according to his good purpose."

The fact is that many, in the name of God, most probably with sincere and good intentions, wrench this verse out of its context. Read the first eleven verses of the chapter. This passage is all about Jesus, all about what He has done for our salvation. Yet, Philippians 2:12 is often used as the basis of a works-based theology, wherein people slave away thinking that at any moment they can lose their salvation. Paul, the author of Philippians, uses the term "work out," and it's a key to understanding this passage. We are to "work out" what God has already "worked in." If God has not already saved us, if He has not already "worked in" our salvation, there is nothing inside us to be "worked out." God places His grace in us so that it might flow out of us into the lives of others.

Finally, you wonder whether we are expected to "perfect" our salvation? Let's pause and consider how we might do such a thing? How could we ever, being given the treasure of salvation, the indwelling of our risen Lord, as "jars of clay" (see 2 Corinthians 4:7), be expected to perfect the eternal riches we have been given? How can we—the perishable, imperfect, and sinful—improve the imperishable, perfect, and holy? We don't perfect what is already perfect. We have been made perfect by Jesus. We are perfected by the atoning work of the cross of the Lamb of God if we accept His sacrifice, completely, without reservation. Hebrews 10:14 says, "By one sacrifice he has made perfect forever those who are being made holy." Ephesians 4:12–13 tells us that Jesus did what He did "to prepare God's people for works of service, so that the body of Christ may be built up until we all reach unity in the faith and in the knowledge of the Son of God and become mature, attaining to the whole measure of the fullness of Christ." Who perfects whom? How do we become perfect? By Jesus, through Jesus, because of Jesus.

DO WE REALLY
HAVE CHOICES?

How free is our free will?

Q   *I believe that God gives each of us free will and that He does not interfere with that free will. However, my wife challenged me about my logic (as she often does). She pointed out that Exodus 9:12 states, "But the LORD hardened Pharaoh's heart and he would not listen to Moses and Aaron, just as the LORD had said to Moses." This seems to imply that God forced Pharaoh's free will to make him do something wrong. There are other examples. On the road to Damascus, Saul became blind to help motivate him to obey God. If he wanted to receive His vision back, he needed to obey God. Not much of a choice, it seems. I guess what bothers me about this is that if God does interfere with free will, then why wouldn't He alter the mind of murderers or child molesters and blind them, so to speak, until they saw the error of their ways?*

A   First, we need to realize our viewpoint. We are looking at an event (Pharaoh hardening his heart) that happened thirty-five hundred years ago. From our twenty-first-century Western mind-set, we're considering a historical event that occurred within the context of the Jewish worldview. We're evaluating the meaning and significance of this event from the perspective of our reality and our language.

So, what does it mean that God hardened Pharaoh's heart? The conclusion first. The moral of this story seems to be that God hardens the hearts of those who harden themselves. Put another way, which comes first—the chicken or the egg? Consider the context of this passage. If you study Exodus chapters 4–14, you will find the term "hardened the heart" (or a similar phrase) used some eighteen times. There are times when the Scripture says that God hardened Pharaoh's heart, and there are times when we read that Pharaoh hardened his own heart. Sometimes the event is recorded passively, such as, Pharaoh's heart *was* hardened. Who initiated the hardening of Pharaoh's heart is not mentioned in such cases.

What happened here, and how do we understand it? About fifteen hundred years after it happened, Paul tried to work through it (Romans 9:14–18), and he was far closer to that time chronologically and culturally than we are. God is, of course, the first cause, the Creator. All that comes after derives from Him. So, since He created Pharaoh, it can easily be said that He hardened Pharaoh's heart, for after all, had God not created humans, no human would ever harden his or her heart. God may have hardened Pharaoh's heart simply because Pharaoh was human. Or God may have added to Pharaoh's hard-hearted, stubborn will by afflicting him with plagues, which caused Pharaoh to be even more resistant. Hebrew culture and worldview accepted such a perspective more than our twenty-first-century Western culture, which glorifies human decision, choice, and independence and does not see our choices as interrelated to God.

Our view in the twenty-first-century Western world is either we have a choice or God has a choice. The ancient Eastern culture tended to see both humans and God as having choices. As an illustration, consider parents and teens. Sometimes the best way for a parent to get a teen to do something is not to make a big deal of the issue—or even to suggest doing the opposite. The recording industry has known for over fifty years that one of the fastest ways to endear teens to music and performers is to revolt their parents. Teens like what turns off and scandalizes their parents. So, who is doing the hardening of the heart in such cases?

Falling out of God's will

Q *I am in college. I think God may have called me to be a teacher. The problem is that I want to pursue other goals. I want to study what I am interested in. But when I stray completely away from education, something horrible always happens. The last time I was considering something other than teaching, my mom had a heart attack. I am afraid something worse is going to happen. I am afraid to have fun. I am afraid to have other interests because I am afraid of falling out of God's will and then something really terrible happening. What do I do? Why is God punishing me?*

A Your question sounds more mystical and superstitious than it does rational and logical. Some Christians believe that God is always waiting around the next corner of life with a big club to beat us over the head. What does the term "falling out of God's will" mean to you? It seems to me, from your question, that you are applying an extremely subjective interpretation to God's will, one based upon fear rather than love.

The fruit of God's Spirit (Galatians 5:22–26) reveals much about God's will for us. I fail to find anything in this list of love, joy, peace, patience, kindness, etc., about fear of God punishing us or about reading God's will into events that happen in our lives or those of loved ones (your mother's heart attack). It would be difficult for me to worship God if I believed that He needed to cause loved ones to have heart attacks in order to get my attention. Such a belief is closer to pagan mythology than it is to biblical truth.

God is not upset when you have fun, when you laugh, or when you smile. God is not mad at you. You may be punishing yourself or you may be punished by concepts about God that others have taught you, but God is not in the business of destroying you and making your life miserable. God is in the salvation and rescue business. He loves everyone, the whole world, according to John 3:16, and did not send Jesus to this world to condemn us, but to save us because He loves us.

How does God lead us?

Q *It seems to me that there is much discussion in some Christian circles concerning the ability to sense God's "leading." For example, "I sensed God's call . . ." or "I prayed and sensed that God wanted me to . . ." or "One of my friends felt led to . . .". I cannot find in the Scriptures where we must "hear" or "sense" God before we can make decisions. As I understand it, we should seek God's "voice" in Scripture.*

A While my background and culture lead me to experience God more in the way you seem to prefer, it is important to give some thought to this topic. Christianity involves the heart and the mind, and our relationship with God is understood and experienced in a variety of ways within Christian faith traditions.

On the one hand, the Bible reveals God to be logical, clear, and coherent. The Bible describes God's message and His intentions as being able to be understood, rather than mysteriously discovered or decoded by those who have secret knowledge.

But God also moves our heart, desires our affection, and tenaciously loves and pursues us. Expressions of how God does this in our lives vary within the denominations of Christianity. And, of course, those experiences of God are expressed through a cultural filter. Some denominations and cultures are more reserved, objective, more focused on the logical knowledge of God, while others are more expressive, subjective, more interested in the personal relationship of knowing God.

There are biblical references to visions, appearances of angels to men and women, conversations of God with humans, etc. Granted, they are more frequent in the Old Testament than the New, but they are there. Many Christians believe that the age of God personally communicating with individual Christians is gone—no longer does God deal with Christians in that way. Others, who would believe that other New Testament gifts of the Holy Spirit, like tongues and divine healing, are still operative within the body of Christ, also believe in a more intimate and immediate relationship with God.

Some Christians, as you note, are fond of talking about God's will and about what God presumably told them to do. They usually speak of God telling them to do something in a metaphorical sense rather than hearing an audible voice. This terminology, however, does offer a convenient, subjective interpretation of the will of God when one can justify that his/her will is one and the same as God's will. I have often kidded with friends who use such a phrase (that God told them to do such and such) that I find their description troubling because God also told me what His will was, and His message to me was the exact opposite of the one He "gave" to my friend!

Of course, when I do so, I make it plain that I am simply trying to convey that I would have healthy skepticism about the absolute truth of what they are saying and that for me God's will must involve more-objective criteria, such as the Bible. On the other hand, I do not want to discount that God can reveal His will to anyone in any way that He might wish to. He does not usually consult me before doing so!

As with many topics, there is probably a balance between these two poles, and it is also probable that no human being is perfectly balanced in seeking to know God. We thank God that He is our heavenly Father and He loves each of us, leading and guiding us as we yield to Him.

PROSPERITY, WORD-FAITH, AND DELIVERANCE

What is the "Word-Faith" and "Prosperity Gospel" all about?

Q *From what I've managed to gather, Word-Faith teaching and the Prosperity Gospel teach that people can achieve wealth, health, and all their other needs simply through faith in God. If that's the case, why is it considered wrong and unscriptural? Third John 1:2 states, "Beloved, I pray that you may prosper in every way and [that your body] may keep well, even as [I know] your soul keeps well and prospers" (AMP). This scripture seems to support prosperity for those who are in Christ, don't you think?*

How about when Jesus said that we shouldn't worry about what to eat or drink but to seek first the kingdom of God? He then went on to say that our heavenly Father knows that we need these things. Wasn't He talking about prosperity? How about Abraham, Job, Solomon, and many other servants of God who were abundantly rich?

A Word-Faith teaching and the Prosperity Gospel are slightly different but exhibit similarities. Word-Faith is the general idea that a person can speak or pray something into existence, the belief that God responds to us only if we recite a mantra-like formula or pray a prayer of "positive confession." According to Word-Faith teaching, God is obligated, once we say and/or do the correct thing, to give us what we want.

Word-Faith teachers cite biblical passages but cite them out of context and abuse them in an effort to prove their teaching, which is, at its foundation, superstition. Word-Faith suggests that our prayers are not answered because we don't have "enough" faith. That teaching leads to oppressive religious legalism when people are convinced that their prayers will be answered if they acquire more faith. In such a case, the goal becomes the acquisition of faith through the vehicles and contrivances of endless rites, rituals, ceremonies, and performance of religious deeds.

The Prosperity Gospel teaches that God's will is for us to be healthy and wealthy. It amounts to selling religious lottery tickets to the weak, sick, and poverty-stricken, who are the ones who are most easily seduced by this teaching. Health-and-wealth churches are extremely popular in inner-city areas of the United States and in disadvantaged, economically challenged areas around the world.

Third John 1:2 is not a promise that all Christians will be healthy and wealthy, but rather it was a normal salutation of a letter at the time John wrote. We might say today, as we write a friend, "I hope you are doing well," or "I pray that all things are going well for you." That's the reason the passage should not be used as a promise of health and wealth. Many who quote this passage erroneously are no doubt unaware of how they are twisting Scripture.

John 10:10, "I have come that they may have life, and have it to the full," is another Prosperity Gospel proof-text favorite that falls apart on logical examination. First of all, none of us will be healthy forever. Sooner or later, each of us will die of disease, accident, or old age. Many devoted Christians are sick. They have horrible health, confined to their beds in hospitals and nursing homes. Many Christians suffer painful and debilitating accidents. Have they done something wrong? The Prosperity Gospel says so. Have they not repented of some secret sin, and when they do will they be delivered from their illness? The health-and-wealth gospel says so. But logic and experience (not to mention the Bible) tell us otherwise.

What about poverty? Is there any biblical promise that Christians will all live lives of luxury on this earth? No, but there are statements about the riches of God's grace. There is a promise that we, by God's grace, become rich because we are the heirs of His kingdom, but all of these statements are about spiritual riches. Once again, the health-and-wealth gospel twists such statements and tries to assure physically poor people that God wants them to be physically rich now. Coincidentally and conveniently, one of the best ways for poor people to get rich quick is to give their money to health-and-wealth preachers. Health-and-wealth preachers often dress well, drive fancy cars, and wear flashy watches and rings because, among other things, if the preacher of health and wealth is not healthy and wealthy, then why should others follow him (or her)?

My church believes in deliverance ministries. What do you think?

Q *Our church has begun heavy use of "deliverance ministries" type materials. I am concerned at this and have begun an in-depth search to come to a better understanding of my own.*

The trouble is although there is a lot of biblically based material in opposition to this ministry view, my church leaders condemn this opposition, saying it comes from people opposed to God's will (whatever that really means!).

My pastor says that I have to be careful reading opposing views because the devil can deceive me. How do I know the truth?

A   As you report, it seems that those who follow some fad or fancy often become dogmatic and judgmental about those who question the wisdom of practices that are at best peripheral to the gospel and at worst contradictory and opposed to the central core teachings of Jesus Christ (see 1 Timothy 1:3–7).

Deliverance ministries put a great deal of emphasis, as you probably know, on the power and work of Satan and his demons. Some insist that we must determine the names or provinces of power of specific demons so that activities like prayer walking, done in an almost primitive, animistic manner, can deliver us from the clutches of the demons. Of course there are many other themes of deliverance ministries having to do with disease, emotional dysfunction, and so on.

It seems that a common technique of some deliverance ministries is to pronounce a problem or difficulty as the work of Satan and then, through manipulative behaviors, pronounce a cure. The cure, of course, is usually attributed to the specific "deliverance" methodology employed by the individual or his/her ministry.

But there is a major theological and biblical difficulty with this teaching, not to mention logical inconsistency. If we are in Christ, we are not in the clutches of Satan. Jesus Christ has delivered those who accept Christ from the clutches of Satan.

The "deliverance ministry" of Jesus Christ did this once and for all. It was accomplished on the cross and as a result of the empty tomb. Jesus has triumphed over death and the grave, over all powers and all principalities. He has already, once and for all, delivered us. To God alone goes the glory for our freedom, not to some deliverance ministry.

There are times when the mere interest in those things that are evil and pernicious can lead to problems that did not exist before. Paul says in Ephesians that we should have nothing to do with the fruitless deeds of darkness, but rather expose them. It is, according to Paul, shameful even to talk about things that are done in secret (Ephesians 5:11–12).

The primary concerns with deliverance ministries:

1. They often give credit to the wrong source. Jesus alone is our Savior, not some method or charismatic leader.

2. For Christians, the emphasis of deliverance ministries is "tilting at windmills." Christ has already, once and for all, delivered us from Satan and his minions.

3. Deliverance ministries often obscure the primary themes of the gospel and send Christians off on wild goose chases, fighting battles that have already been won. As a result, Christians often fail to address and stress the central and core beliefs of Christianity while off on deliverance crusades.

4. The act of becoming involved with deliverance ministries often results in individuals believing that they now have problems that they never had. Real or imagined, those involved with deliverance ministries often find that they lived a less complicated and problematic life in Christ before they knew that there was such a thing as "deliverance ministry." The Bible gives us the standard of measuring such activities by their fruit.

5. Deliverance ministries often become the watershed

issue for those involved, and those who have little time for such a ministry are often condemned and judged by advocates of deliverance ministries as being self-righteous, legalistic, uncaring, unspiritual, or perhaps not even converted at all. Once again, we should look to the fruit of such practices.

CULTS

Driving Miss Mormon

Q *What should Christians do when a loved one comes under the influence of a cult? I was secure in thinking my child understood Christianity and had accepted Jesus. She grew up in Christian churches and is now a young adult. I believe she was sincere in her acceptance of Christ, but now she has decided to become a Mormon. I know, having been a Mormon, the power that they exert over their members and the power they have to tear families apart in the name of God. I don't want this to happen in our family. How do I support her but yet not support the cult she is in? I am at a loss as to how to handle this. Is there anything that I can do or avoid doing—i.e., what if she needs a ride to church? Do I give her the ride or say no? I know that this scenario sounds a bit silly, but these little things can blow up into battles beyond repair. How does a Christian show Christian love in these kinds of circumstances?*

A It has often been said that cults are the left-behind baggage of the church. They feed on and grow because of inadequate teaching and misplaced priorities in Christianity at large. This does not necessarily mean that everyone who is attracted by such a group would never have been interested had some Christian only done a better job, for that would be a legalistic conclusion. But it does mean we can look into the mirror of our own faith and practice as we search for answers.

Based upon my understanding and experiences, I have several comments about the situation you face:

1. Ultimatums may only drive your daughter more deeply into Mormonism.

2. Don't withhold love or acceptance based upon your daughter's choice. God loves us with an everlasting and unconditional love. Ask God to help you give this kind of love to your daughter. It is essential that you maintain and even build your relationship with your daughter, for, as you say, many cultic teachings are dedicated to breaking down the relationships we treasure.

3. Driving your daughter to a Mormon church may seem spiritually unethical, but if she is going to go anyway, perhaps you can make a point of doing other errands so that driving her is not your only mission as you pull out of your driveway. Is this where the battle should be fought; is this where you need to draw the line in the sand?

4. Be careful about doctrinal arguments, for, as you will recall from your own past experiences, those who are being indoctrinated by a cult are taught to expect opposition. Doctrinal arguments from loved ones may actually reinforce to the potential cult member that they must be doing the right thing because family members, friends, and loved ones are arguing with them.

5. In some ways, this situation is a little like the tightrope that a parent walks when their teenager brings home someone of the opposite sex of whom the parent disapproves. If you disapprove too much, or even at all, you know you run the risk of

your teen befriending the person of whom you disapprove simply because you disapprove. This does not mean that we never disapprove, but it does mean that disapproval communicated to a young adult demands far greater skills of tact and wisdom than needed when that same child was six or seven years of age.

Haunted by cult guilt

Q *I spent twenty years as a Jehovah's Witness. My problem is that I still have dreams and feelings of guilt for robbing my ex-husband's parents (who are now deceased) of all the holidays my husband and I refused to celebrate because we followed Watchtower teachings. My ex was an only child. Ten years after I became a Witness, he also became one. After his parents died, for various reasons, I left the marriage and am now remarried and a member of a Christian church. My ex is still a JW. I can't get rid of the feeling that I have. His parents were very patriotic, and my husband gave up that belief when he became a Witness. Now I am celebrating birthdays, holidays, and national holidays—but with a lot of guilt. If my ex could see me now, he would be sickened that I "returned to the vomit," as he would put it. I feel "icky" inside because of the pain I caused from living the beliefs I once had. I love my current husband immensely. This is a good marriage. But the past haunts me where I cannot fully enjoy my new relationship with Jesus without feeling like I am doing something wrong.*

A When a person who was once trapped in cultic teaching realizes the enormous errors they accepted and the practical life decisions that were influenced by bogus teaching, there is a great deal of regret and grief. Those who leave a group who claimed to be the exclusive, one-and-only "true church" are in pain. They experience the loss of many close and beloved friends, most of whom will not even talk with them, for former cult members who have renounced cultic teaching are usually shunned by the group they once regarded as their spiritual family.

Life within a cultic group can be somewhat like living in a false, alternative universe. Cultic groups have a culture all their own. They offer alternative social lives; they offer safety from "the world." Some cultic groups refuse to allow "inter-marriage" with "outsiders," so the world of potential spouses, and thus social life that can lead to marriage, is severely limited.

Cults often offer previously disaffected, disenfranchised, and dysfunctional people an accepting environment—a family-like atmosphere many new converts have never experienced before. The idea and imagery of family is commonly used in cultic movements to speak of the larger entity and the prerequisite obedience and loyalty one should give to that family. It is no accident that cult leaders and their immediate subordinates encourage or at least "allow" themselves to be spoken of in paternalistic and maternalistic terms. Cultic groups offer a false sense of unity, a false sense of a unique and special place in the world as well as one's relationship with God. There is often a false sense of history as it is often revised by cult leaders to fit the new reality they offer.

Because cults demand allegiance, they demand a new life, which effectively ends the former life of new converts. Cult members often have no option but to burn all bridges in their past, including career, education, professional affiliations, family, and friends. Then, when a cult member leaves the false environment in which they have lived, they can experience feelings of grief (because of their losses), anger (because of what they see as their gullibility in allowing themselves to accept falsehoods), and enormous regret at what they believe their lives could have been had they not been consumed and defined by the cultic movement.

Former cult members are often astonished at how they believed themselves to be elitist and exclusive, better than anyone and everyone. As they look back on life within a cult, they see the incredible isolation and often have major challenges adjusting to a normal society and culture. It can take some former cult members years to escape the overwhelming judgmentalism and condemnation of others (as well as themselves) that permeates cultic life. Former cult members can have problems accepting reality, as cultic life often involves a denial of reality, with culture shock being experienced as they either re-enter society or enter it for the first time. Think of Rip Van Winkle awaking from a long slumber. Some have described the shock they experienced at entering the real world after a cultic experience as leaving a cave and rubbing their eyes because of the light or as leaving a climate-controlled room and experiencing weather for the first time.

Some believe, based on studies of former cult members, that it may take up to eight years for former cult members to integrate into society at large. Some believe that we never get over our past, and in some ways, regardless of the kind of past we have had, this is a true statement. In *Requiem for a Nun*, William Faulkner had one of his characters say, "The past is never dead. It's not even past."

The guilt you speak of is also a real and present spiritual enemy for all of us, but especially so for those who have recently escaped from the swamps of cultic teaching. Survivor guilt haunts some who were able to escape. Those who made it out of cultic teaching and belief may ask, "Why me?" while many former friends continue to be held captive spiritually with seemingly no hope for an escape. Sometimes guilt is experienced because the former cult member can't really believe that they are free—free to, in your case, celebrate birthdays, salute the flag, celebrate Thanksgiving, or worship God at Christmas and Easter. Even though they know that certain prohibited activities, food or drink, or behaviors are not wrong, they often feel guilt when drinking a Coke, eating meat, wearing cosmetics or jewelry, or giving blood.

And there is tremendous guilt, such as you speak of, when family members are considered—when one thinks of what was denied and missed, what young people could not participate in or qualify for given the restrictions of a cult.

Many former cult members have found that they have "graduated" from a great deal of the pain, sense of loss, anger, and regret when, by God's grace, they learn to accept their own past—that it happened, that it will not change, and that to some degree it will shape the rest of their lives. Such a step can enable them to move beyond regret and remorse about what might have been, about what their children could have done, about the family holidays that could have been enjoyed, about the community and family involvement that could have been enjoyed.

Sooner or later, forgiveness comes into this picture—forgiveness of self for having swallowed unbiblical teachings hook, line, and sinker; forgiveness of others in the cultic movement who also were deceived and passed on bad teaching and contributed to painful experiences. Often a former cult member blames God, so God is also part of forgiveness. And it is in this experience many find a real relationship with their loving Lord, with Jesus who died for them on His cross (a cross that is so denied by some cults they refuse to use the term but instead substitute the word *stake*). Who are we to forgive God as if God needs forgiveness? But in our pain and anger, we often blame God, and in this search many come to know God as they never have before.

Recovering from legalistic, authoritarian oppression in the name of God is complete when the real Jesus is discovered, when a relationship with Jesus takes the place of a relationship with a cult, when authentic Christianity is experienced, when growth in the grace and knowledge of our Lord takes place. Replace the guilt, shame, pain, anguish, and rage with Jesus, who bears all of our sin, who takes our own burdens, and returns to us His divine rest. Rest in Him! Come to know Him! Enjoy Him! Trust Him! Replace the fear and manipulation of cultic teaching with the love of God, which passes all understanding.

Remember that great passage in Romans 8:1: "There is no condemnation for those who are in Christ Jesus." All of your guilt and shame, all of the condemnation you have felt, is gone in and through the blood of Jesus. Let it go, for it is gone. You are white as snow, free in Christ, and no human can condemn you. "If God is for us, who can be against us?" (Romans 8:31).

CHRISTIAN JARGON

Do I need to learn and use "Christian-ese"?

Q *I'm finding it hard to communicate with some of the Christians I have met. No one I know talks the way people do in the church I am attending. Can you help?*

A There are several schools of thought about in-house Christian vocabulary. On the one hand, there are technical terms, as with any discipline or endeavor, needed to accurately define Christian belief and practice. Using specific terminology enables us to be concise and accurate, and to avoid misunderstanding.

Here's a few technical terms that are necessary to accurately explain some of the complexities of the Christian faith:

Atonement
Eschatology
Hermeneutics
Incarnation
Justification
Sanctification

On the other hand, if we wish to reach a wider audience than our own holy huddles, then we will attempt to contextualize Christian faith and practice into the common language of our day and age. Many people, Christians and non-Christians alike, do not relate to the technical terminology of Christianity. There might be times when they need to learn it, but there are times when its use might be a negative, for the terms simply fly over the top of their heads and little or no real communication takes place.

There are also times when imprecise clichés gain a wide following and become a barrier for anyone who is outside of the particular Christian "club" that favors the use of such terms and phrases. "Christian-ese" is an appropriate description of this sublanguage, and while it may have meaning for insiders and initiates, to others it represents a communication barrier rather than a bridge. Here are a few examples of "Christian-ese" that I personally find unnecessary and perhaps even elitist:

Ask Jesus into your heart
Claim the blood
Coming up alongside
Feeding on the Word
Having a burden
Journeying mercies
"Just"—as in "Lord, we "just" thank You for . . .
Lift Jesus up
Share your testimony
Witness

Finally, there are obsolete terms that come primarily from the King James Version of 1611 that seem to make people feel more religious if they use them. But once again, they are dated and have meaning only for a select few, and certainly do not communicate with twenty-first-century humanity. Along with the obvious "thees" and "thous" here are a few additional examples:

Admonition
Backslide
Concupiscence
Doleful
Kindred
Mammon
Smite
Surety

Using a modern Bible translation can help with the obsolete language. As far as "Christian-ese," I believe it helps to explain to others that the terminology they are using seems narrow and provincial, and that "normal" vocabulary will enhance effective communication. As far as technical terms, we have to understand that there are accurate and precise terms that must be used to avoid misunderstandings.

BAPTISM

Infant baptism—not good enough?

Q *I was baptized as an infant by my grandfather. I confirmed my faith in the Presbyterian church when I was fifteen years of age. My wife was baptized in the Baptist church by immersion. She does not believe in infant baptism and does not think that our son should be baptized at birth. I am having problems explaining infant baptism to my wife.*

Second problem: My wife and I joined a nondenominational church. When we joined, they asked if I had accepted Jesus Christ and if I had been baptized. I said yes to both questions, and we became members. They later realized that my baptism was at birth. They pulled my membership and would like for me to be immersed in order to become a member again. I am really struggling with this. I know that any relationship with God could be improved, but I do not feel compelled to be re-baptized, nor do I think being baptized again will necessarily please God. Luckily, my wife supports me no matter what. I find it hypocritical that a church is "nondenominational" but will not allow a fellow Christian to join "their" church without "their" accepted baptism ritual.

A   Your question concerns the mode of baptism, an issue that has divided Christians for hundreds of years. It seems that you and your wife have knowingly and intelligently joined a nondenominational church so that minor, nonessential issues will not cause the two of you to lose sight of your common heritage (your commitment in marriage to each other and your spiritual commitment to the body of Christ). Insignificant issues can trouble friendships and marriages. If allowed to grow, these minor issues can morph from molehills into mountains. Your reasoning seems to be sound and based on the Bible. Do not allow anyone to turn your freedom in Christ into religious ritualism.

There is no direct command to baptize infants, but neither is there a prohibition. The biblical example is that God works in families, and thus we have whole households being baptized (Cornelius in Acts). Jesus blesses children, Jesus is conceived of the Holy Spirit, and John the Baptist is filled with the Holy Spirit from the womb. Jesus warns against offending the little ones (while it has a spiritual meaning, there is much significance and relevance in this teaching directed to our child neglecting and abusing society). For its part, immersion has many biblical precedents: Jesus' own baptism, the meaning of the Greek word translated *baptism* (immersion), word pictures that Paul offers of the grave and of baptism as we come out of both to new life, etc.

Central to this issue, however, is the fact that while we are commanded to be baptized, the act of baptism does not save. The act and the ongoing process of spiritual salvation is an intimate and personal relationship between an individual and his/her God. No church administers baptism that saves versus an inferior baptism practiced by another denomination that fails to save. No pastor or church has biblical authority to demand re-baptism when someone who is already baptized joins their church. As for a child being baptized or not, it is not a critical issue if the child is not baptized as an infant. It is equally wrong to assume that children will not be saved unless they are baptized, which is a popular view of what infant baptism confers. The families of both parents and the parents themselves are usually the center of such controversies.

What if I die before I'm baptized?

Q *I am concerned that I could die before I get a chance to be baptized. While I want to be baptized, if I were to die before baptism, does that mean I'm lost?*

A Salvation is a personal matter between God and each one of us. No formal or informal act, rite, or ritual saves us. We, of course, do come to repentance, we ask God for forgiveness, and we accept Jesus Christ and commit our lives to Him. We can do that ourselves, or we can do that in the company of others. In any case, subsequent to our acceptance of Jesus Christ and our trust in God's love for us, God saves us.

Baptism is commanded of Christians, but believer's baptism (adult baptism) in the vast majority of cases is an action that is taken by an individual after the individual accepts Christ and is saved. The idea that we might die before we get baptized or perform some other religious ritual or deed and that therefore we will be lost forever is manipulative and smacks of man-made religious coercion more than it does of authentic Christianity.

Isn't accepting Christ enough?
Why be baptized?

Q *I want to know if I must be baptized to go to heaven. Is just accepting Christ in my life enough?*

A There is nothing that you must do in order to go to heaven other than the one prerequisite of accepting the grace that God offers, the Savior who alone can save you and the Lord who alone is worthy of your worship. No other act is "required." However, the Bible does direct those whom God saves to be baptized, not as a ticket into heaven but as an act on the part of an individual to signify what God has done and their acceptance of Jesus Christ as Lord and Savior.

The specific manner, type, or mode of baptism, the age at which it is administered, the amount of water that is used, and the church or pastor or priest who conducts the ceremony is not, according to the Bible, relevant to our salvation.

Baptism—is once enough?

Q *How many times should a person be baptized? In my case, I was baptized as an infant in the Catholic church. But I'm grown now and I'm not Catholic. I was baptized in the Seventh Day Adventist church a few years back, but now I don't agree with their beliefs so I have left. I'm now attending a Baptist church. I don't believe I should be baptized again just because I changed churches. When I was baptized as an adult, I did it knowing why and what it means to me as a Christian, and I think that's all that matters.*

A I would generally agree with the way you seem to be leaning regarding this question. First, we are commanded to be baptized, but there is no command to be re-baptized. Once is enough. There is no reason why someone should feel a need to be baptized again. If an individual decides to be baptized again, that individual should realize their re-baptism is by choice, not by necessity. Generally speaking, in terms of baptism, "once is enough." Multiple baptisms simply cast doubt on the integrity and ability of God's promise. God's work is not limited by who does the baptism or by the mode of baptism.

Most re-baptisms are of those who were baptized as infants and later come to believe in what is called "believer's baptism"—the idea that surely one ought to know what one is doing and the commitment one is making at the time of this sacrament.

As you state, there certainly is no need to be re-baptized simply because you changed churches. No church should insist on re-baptism as a condition of membership, for the conversion experience is not necessarily one and the same as baptism. Becoming a child of God most certainly is not one and the same as being baptized by a specific church; churches and pastors do not confer/award/give conversion. Churches and pastors can and should help an individual to know what God is doing, and in many cases has already done, in an individual's life. But to appropriate and define conversion to a set of denominational doctrinal beliefs is overstepping the responsibility of the ministry of Jesus Christ. No human has the authority to direct you to be re-baptized.

Baptism signifies rebirth and regeneration, but it does not

convey or confer rebirth. The power of baptism is not in water, or how much water, or the method of baptism, or the person doing the baptizing, or the church under whose auspices the baptism is done, but in the power that belongs to God alone.

Baptism is an outward sign, a profession of faith that is made by the believer (or in the case of infant baptism, by the infant's family and church family) that testifies to the commitment that the believer is making. It is, in some ways, like a wedding ceremony, a formal commitment. Baptism may be done by immersion or by sprinkling. Although Christians are free to differ about the mode of baptism, as Christians we should not declare spiritual superiority because of the mode we favor. Many Protestants point to the baptism of Jesus and note that He was immersed. Other Protestants and Catholics will note that several entire households were baptized in the New Testament, and this would have included infants who presumably would not have been immersed.

Baptism is the sign of God's promise of salvation, and the fact that we give our lives to Him, and that we accept this salvation, and the grace by which and through which He gives us eternal life.

WEIRD RELIGIOUS
STUFF IN THE
NAME OF GOD

What's this gold dust thing all about?

Q *I have recently been in a debate over the "gold dust" phenomenon, where gold dust is said to appear on worshippers in certain settings and is thought to be a manifestation or sign from God. I have talked to many people who swear by this so-called gold dust. One friend said she had an experience that she knows was from the Holy Spirit when she indeed received some gold dust. While I squirmed, not knowing what to say, I kept wondering what Jesus really meant by His statement that we'd have the same power He had, to do even greater things. Does this really include raising people from the dead, turning water into wine, or walking on water? Where in the Bible do Christians get "permission" to be slain in the spirit or experience this gold dust thing?*

On the other hand, if a miracle happens that has never before been experienced, or there's no precedent for it in Scripture, does that automatically make the whole thing un-Christian? Or can God, indeed, do something new in the church today that can be considered legitimate? I know everyone wants to live powerfully for Christ, but how much miracle-producing power did He really give to you and me?

A The idea that Jesus taught us that we would be able to do all of the things He did and even more is a paraphrase; in fact, it is a misunderstanding. Jesus did say that we would do "greater things" (John 14:12), but for anyone to teach that Jesus had miracles, physical manifestations, and carnival-like tricks in mind is twisting and misrepresenting Scripture.

The Gospel of John is about spiritual life, new life, the resurrected life of Christ. John does not tell us that we will all receive dramatic physical healing, that all Christians will see incredible visions, that all Christians will do or experience dramatic miracles. John is talking about the life of the age to come, about the fact that when we accept Jesus we cross over from this life of the flesh to eternity in Christ (John 5:24). We dare not reduce this precious teaching about eternal life, the supreme and matchless gift of eternal life, and minimize it into some kind of carnival sideshow that is here and now, based upon emotion and feeling. Christians suffer in the Bible, in history, as well as in this contemporary world. Christianity is not one big experiential orgy of emotion and feeling, filled with miracles, dramatic interventions, or generous portions of gold dust for that matter.

Some of the most mature Christians suffer pain, heartache, and poverty all their lives. They never get healed at the "Wednesday evening healing service." They never handle snakes, they never get gold dust in their teeth, and they never bark like a dog or get slain in the spirit. Why? Because all that stuff is neither here nor there; in fact, more often than not it is "out there," on the fringes of the gospel of Jesus Christ.

What's the point of all this hype and emotionalism? Do we come closer to God through manifestations? Do we come to know our Lord in a new and profound way? Or do we find that we simply have a sensory experience based solely upon feelings? And what happens when the circus folds up its tents and leaves town? What is left in its wake? Disillusionment and loss of trust in God—God who has been misrepresented. Jesus suggests we will know the work of pastors, teachers, and ministries by their fruit (Matthew 7:15–23).

Of course, God can do something new; He is always at work doing just that. But the new things that God does are always, first and foremost, based on our spiritual lives with Him—with any physical evidence, manifestations, or miracles as secondary and comparatively unimportant. The biggest miracle of all, after all, is for God to change the human heart.

Jesus taught His disciples to "take up his cross and follow me" (Matthew 16:24). Isn't it rather ironic that people actually go to a "crusade" or "revival" in the name of Jesus Christ and believe He is going to rain down gold dust on them and make them healthy and wealthy?

More spiritually mature than you are . . .

Q *My ex-pastor told me that she and her husband were "farther up the mountain" than I was, so she was going to help make my wife and me better Christians. What is to be our view toward new converts or even non-Christians? We are all at different levels, but is Christianity comparable to "moving up the corporate ladder," or does the kingdom of God use a different "grading" system? Do we receive a greater reward or better placement in heaven than those farther behind us do? This lady claimed to have a vision where she saw Jesus giving the saints their crowns, but He plucked various jewels from those Christians' crowns who she said had not repented of sin in their lives.*

Is the idea that since someone has been saved longer than I have been or helped lead more people to Jesus, that they have built themselves up greater treasures in heaven than the thief who died with Jesus on the cross?

A Thank God that He has given you His gift of grace as well as a sense of humor! Your point, given as rhetorical statements, is well stated. You let the silly, illogical, and unreasonable arguments of your former church and pastor fall on their face by restating them.

Churches and religious leaders who cast doubt on our personal relationship with God often do so, whether knowingly or unknowingly, for the purpose of controlling and manipulating us. One of the ways to ensure that all of the seats/chairs/pews will be filled on Sunday morning is to keep people in a perpetual state of felt need and insecurity. The problem with such an approach is obvious; Jesus died for us for virtually the exact opposite reason. He died for us to free us from stuff like that.

The whole idea of "I'm better than you are, more spiritually mature" is a contrivance which endeavors to keep people in religious debt. Jesus said on the cross, "The debt is paid." There is no grading system such as the one this person describes, nor is the vision that was related to you in line with Holy Scripture. It should therefore be rejected.

THE UNPARDONABLE
SIN

I am not sure Jesus has forgiven me.

Q *I am currently in a dangerous situation, according to my
Christian friends. Can God help a person who cannot
repent? I constantly fear that I have committed the "unpardonable
sin." The Bible says that those who commit the sin of blasphemy
against the Holy Spirit will never be forgiven. How can God
soften a heart that has gone hard? I have traumatized all my
Christian friends, and they tell me to repent. I am trying to, but
I need a new heart for it. Can Jesus give me a new heart and soul?
I have repeatedly asked for His forgiveness, but I am not sure if I
am forgiven. Does He forgive me? My father says, "The Lord
understands everyone and is willing to forgive everything." I
would sincerely love forgiveness from God from this terrible thing,
and I am trying to fix my hard heart but I cannot. Is Jesus the one
to do the job? And if so, how can I trust in Him?*

A How have you become convinced that you cannot
repent? Perhaps, for the sake of example, the specific
problem that has led to this dangerous situation is alcoholism.
Perhaps you are convinced that you cannot repent because you

cannot kick this habit. However, the fact that you can't overcome an addiction would not be proof that you are refusing to repent and that you are blaspheming God. It may be proof that you need medical help as you don't seem to be able to deal with the addiction by yourself.

Those who are not forgiven are those who essentially choose not to be forgiven, by refusing to ask for and accept forgiveness. God always forgives. But we must ask for and accept His forgiveness. Those who are not forgiven do not wish to be forgiven. They are not forgiven because they do not ask for or accept forgiveness. Such individuals may have come to the place where they acknowledge no power other or higher than themselves so they may reason, "What's the use of asking someone equal to or less than yourself to forgive you?"

You seem to think that your heart was once "soft" but is now "hard." Perhaps it is. Perhaps it never was "soft"—if you mean changed and softened by spiritual rebirth. You say that your Christian friends are telling you to repent. Again, they may be correct in that you should cease the kind of activity and behavior you have referenced. However, as I mention above, perhaps you do not have the ability, without help, to deal with the massive problem(s) that face you. It's much easier to pass out glib advice, telling someone to get their life together, than it is to be that person and understand exactly what may be involved in getting a life together.

Yes, Jesus can give you a new heart; He can give you a new life. Yes, He forgives you. He is willing to forgive anything. Nothing shocks Him. Whatever you have done, no matter how bad you are, or think you are, God has seen it all before. He will forgive you. Don't let the idea that "God is so offended by my sin that He will never have anything to do with me again" stop you from going to God and asking for His love, mercy, and forgiveness.

You may need professional help, depending on the nature of this situation. Your parents and good friends may be able to support and stand by you as you seek such help. Don't avoid getting help because you are afraid of letting family or friends down. We are all human. We are all weak and strong in differing ways. It seems you may need help in a specific way. So please take the steps necessary to find and obtain it.

HOMOSEXUALITY

Homosexuality—when Christians sin again

Q *I'm a recovered homosexual. I was saved a couple years ago and was ready to live my new life, but I slipped up and committed that sin again, which led me to think that I was hopeless. Is there any hope for me? I've confessed the sin, recommitted my life to Christ, have had no desire even to go back to the old way, but I still feel guilty.*

A The reality is that Christians live new spiritual lives, lives of the age to come because of the fact that Jesus lives His risen life in us. That is our spiritual reality. We are now seated with Christ in heavenly places (Ephesians 2:6), while at the same time our physical reality means that we are still in this body of flesh. As Christians, we sin because we are in the flesh (1 John 1:8). That will never change until we go to heaven or until this body is transformed into an incorruptible one (1 Corinthians 15).

While Christians occasionally sin, we do not sin habitually, for then we would not be Christians, by definition. Galatians 5 tells us that Christ in us produces fruit—fruit that is part of

154

being His workmanship. There are times when we will sin, but that sin will not characterize our new life.

You are not hopeless; you are a child of God. Of course there is hope for you, just like there is for all other Christians.

We are saved by grace. That means God loves us just as much right now as He ever will or ever has. Our actions do not manipulate God into loving us more or less. Grace sounds unbelievable for Christians and has a hint of scandal—that is, it seems to humans that we might take advantage of God. God knows that, of course.

We are saved by grace even though grace may initially seem to us to be a loophole that allows us to do what we want when we want and still be forgiven. But the more we walk with God—the more our love to Him is a response to the love He lavishes on us—the more it seems ludicrous, immature, and un-Christian to attempt to play grace as a trump card anytime we want to get away with something.

You sound, from this brief message, as if you love God with all your heart and soul. Those who willfully turn their backs on God believe that God will not and perhaps even cannot forgive them. Furthermore, they do not wish to avail themselves of God's forgiveness. It is the ultimate blasphemy against God, a refusal to believe. You sound to me as if you believe with all your heart that Jesus alone can save you and that He has. Rest in that. Seek God and follow Him. He will never forsake you.

Alienated from other Christians

 I've been homosexual most all my life. I accepted Christ and became a Christian in 1989. My relationship with

God is deep and true, but this homosexual temptation embarrasses me and separates me in my heart and mind from the family of God. I'm starved for Christian fellowship. I've come to realize that I've developed only a few deep relationships with other Christians because of this. I don't believe anyone even suspects that I'm dealing with this same-sex attraction, and I've only told a select few Christians about my struggle; they were all shocked. My experience has been that all too often Christians have harsh feelings toward homosexuals. I've overheard many such conversations from those who never suspected that I was struggling with this. I keep silent about my struggle primarily for two reasons: to protect my reputation and to protect the sense of safety of those around me. What hope is there for Christians like me to have deep relationships with other Christians?

A   Thank you for your heartfelt insights. You are correct, of course. Unfortunately, many Christians have allowed homosexuality to be characterized as the worst sin, and to condemn, lampoon, stereotype, and even speak maliciously of those who struggle with this particular sin of the flesh.

There are many sins of the flesh, but somehow liars and gluttons don't receive the same vilification from many churches and individual Christians. The wisdom of the old adage of "hating the sin but loving the sinner" is often preached but not followed. And you are correct; many homosexual Christians are forced to maintain silence for their own good and for their immediate family and friends. As Christians we wish this were not the case, but it is, and undoubtedly you have been wise in many of the decisions you have made about protecting yourself and those you love. But as you note, lack of support and fellowship is something you must deal with.

You, and others like you, have our prayers. We are often encouraged to pray for persecuted Christians in such places as China, North Korea, and Saudi Arabia. We pray for Palestinian Christians who are caught in a no-man's land between the Jews and their predominantly Islamic fellow Palestinians. But we should not forget to pray for those Christians who have a real and meaningful relationship with God, who resist homosexuality, and refuse to act out the behavior. Ironically, these Christians live with a struggle that they believe must remain secret, largely because of the animosity and prejudice of their fellow Christians.

Is homosexuality a sin or a sickness?

Q *Some Christians, while not accepting homosexuality as a normal behavior, characterize it as a sickness, whose victims are in need of treatment or rehabilitation, rather than a sin. What is your opinion?*

A The Bible is clear about the practice of homosexuality. It is a sin. Just like other sins—no more, no less. If we conclude that homosexuality is deserving of victimhood, and so canonize it as an illness, then we must similarly address all other biblically defined sins. The end of this exercise in self-pity and self-justification will be the conclusion that we are all victims, we are all sick, but we are not sinners. Following this line of reasoning, we will conclude that we are all "okay"—we don't need a Savior; at best we need a little treatment.

Such a conclusion is not only unbiblical, it is also illogical and an act of denial.

Some will try to link the biblical mandates against homosexuality with Scripture passages dealing with slavery. They point out the fact that Christians once saw little if any problem with human slavery and that Christianity itself finally became a major force in the abolition of slavery. Such individuals note that it's only a matter of time before Christianity will see how ill-informed and bigoted it has been, and it will then accept the practice of homosexuality.

This is an apples-and-oranges comparison. The practice of homosexuality is condemned in both the Old and New Testaments, in spite of cultural acceptance in some areas of the civilized world. While slavery was allowed in the Old Testament and the evil of slavery is not addressed or repudiated in the New Testament, we do not find any New Testament ethical imperative that normalizes slavery. The unavoidable conclusion, at least in hindsight, of the power of the cross of Christ is that human slavery would eventually cease within Christian cultures. No similar reasonable conclusion can be made regarding homosexual practice.

The Bible does not condemn the practice of homosexuality as the worst of all sins. However, there is no way that the Bible can be contorted or compromised into blessing a contrivance, because a contrivance makes us feel better, agrees with us, or in some way matches politically correct notions of our society. Homosexuality is a sin, not an illness, according to the Bible.

HEALING

Praying for healing

Q *I am deaf and communicate via American sign language. I have a question about healing. I would like to know if my pastor and church should pray and fast for my healing, or should I pray and fast for myself? I have been to healing crusades of some famous evangelists. I do not want to say anything against them in case they are for real, but I suspect they are not for real. I decided to go straight to Jesus Christ and ask for my healing. I want to know what is scriptural and what is not scriptural about healing.*

A There is no reason that anyone should feel prohibited from praying for the healing of anything or anyone. "Nothing is impossible with God" (Luke 1:37).

However, physical healing is not the primary kind of healing that Jesus brings. He did heal many in His earthly ministry, but He did not heal everyone in need. The book of Acts records some who had been in Jerusalem at the time of Jesus but were not physically healed by Jesus; instead they received healing from God via the ministry of the apostles. Jesus' healing is first and foremost spiritual, giving release, redemption, and reconciliation from the power of sin and death. He delivers us from spiritual bondage, superstition, ignorance, and fear.

Unfortunately, religion, even in His name, often seeks to bring us into spiritual bondage so that it can control us. But Paul says to us clearly, "It is for freedom that Christ has set us free. Stand firm, then, and do not let yourselves be burdened again by a yoke of slavery" (Galatians 5:1).

God obviously does not heal everyone of the physical diseases, dysfunctions, and problems they face. Many Christians live with ongoing suffering and pain. Paul gives himself as an example, telling us that he fervently sought healing, on three separate occasions, but God's answer was no. Paul concludes that God was telling him, "My grace is sufficient for you, for my power is made perfect in weakness." Paul then comments, "Therefore I will boast all the more gladly about my weaknesses, so that Christ's power may rest on me. . . . For when I am weak, then I am strong" (2 Corinthians 12:9–10).

I don't know when or whether God will physically heal you and give you the gift of hearing. No human knows that, only God. God determines what is best for each of us, given His perfect love for us. No one should give you the expectation that God will heal you in return for some action or behavior on your part—if only you do certain things, if only you obey better and more, if only you perform duties and responsibilities, or if you attend the right healing crusade. This is not the message of the gospel of Jesus Christ. The gospel says that God spiritually heals all who come to Jesus Christ, all who accept God's grace, which is sufficient for our salvation. The gospel does not give us guarantees of physical healing. The gospel does not say that the "best Christians" will not suffer or experience pain. The gospel, in fact, implies that we are called to pick up our cross and follow Jesus. God loves each and every one of us and will work in our lives in His wisdom, mercy, and love—though we may not always understand or appreciate how He is working or how much He loves us.

So, yes, by all means pray. Pray for healing. Pray for others. Pray that you might come to know God in ways that you have not. Pray that God will use you as a tool in His hands.

LEGALISM

Just what do you mean by "legalism"?

Q *I have heard the term* legalism *used many times, always negatively. What exactly does it refer to?*

A As used within Christianity, legalism generally implies the keeping of the law (however the law might be defined, interpreted, and understood), assuming that obedience to law earns eternal merit and favor from God. Other terms for this mind-set, such as Galatianism and Judaism, refer to specific practices the New Testament denounces. Legalism, according to the gospel of grace, essentially comes down to this: there are two ways to deal with human sin and culpability. One, generally called grace, is to accept the sacrifice Jesus Christ offers to us without price. The other, generally called legalism, is to attempt to justify oneself by virtue of one's good deeds and works.

Breaking free from legalism

Q *I am a married mother of three. As I look back, I realize that I grew up in a very legalistic home. By this, I mean that I was taught to keep "holy habits" so that I could be worthy* *of my salvation as well as dodge the discipline and scorn of my church elders. I realize now that I was really participating in spiritual idolatry. Somewhere along the line, I stopped looking to God for His love and started looking to man. Oh, how I loved being a "better Christian" than all the rest.*

Well, my world started to unravel this winter. One thing our church has always made perfectly clear is that a large family is not something to be desired. They say that the less children couples have, the more benefit they are to the work of God (which is one and the same as the work of this particular church). When I became pregnant with my third child, the assistant pastor asked us, "Well, we're kind of surprised about this. Don't you guys use birth control?" My husband and I were so flabbergasted by this question we didn't even respond.

I had the strange feeling that something was coming undone in my life, something that we needed to get over and leave behind us. On Easter Sunday, I was recovering from surgery and my husband took our children to another church for a change. Well, my husband came home excited—and he never comes home from church excited. We have gone to this new church several times now, and I am in a spin. The people in this church look "worldly" to me, the music is contemporary, they use a modern translation of the Bible, and every time I attend I can't stop crying for joy. This is the first place I ever heard about God's grace and justification. The pastor preached a few weeks ago about how when we accept Jesus, He does the work from the inside out, and when we try to fix it from the outside in, we end up with an infection. The minute he said that, I realized I was infected.

My husband is seriously contemplating switching churches, and I am in a quandary. My current church is authoritarian. You must measure up to their standards. Here's my struggle: I have never believed in all these legalistic standards, but now, I don't know if I can live without them. They have been a security blanket for me. Whenever I didn't feel worthy enough or perfect enough, I would just recall my long skirt or makeup-less face and then would feel secure in "my" salvation. This new church is different, but I love not being judged the whole time I'm there.

After our latest visit to the new church, my husband turned to me and said, "You know, I don't know how to worship God." I feel like my theology is all messed up. To be honest, I don't really know anything about my theology. My husband and I are terrified that if we leave our church for this new church, we, along with our children, will burn in hell. It even sounds ridiculous when I type it, but it is the truth. We just don't know what to do.

A   There is no doubt that you are bogged down in legalistic religion, and you and your husband need to be free in Christ (Galatians 5:1) from all of the human rules and regulations that have you in bondage. No leader, in the name of Christ, has the right to give you and your husband authoritarian directives and intimidation about the size of your family. Those decisions are between you, your husband, and God. We are free to seek advice from qualified professionals we trust, of course, but it seems like the "advice" you were given was forced, in the name of God.

Your description of your dilemma makes it crystal clear that you know that you have been manipulated, controlled, and condemned, and that you are anything but free in Christ.

Unfortunately, there are churches that make it extremely hard to leave—and they do this in the name of Christ—with guilt trips, family pressure, and threats of hellfire. But this one point alone is a sign that all is not well, for the body of Christ is not contained by one church. There are Christians in many different churches, and there are many reasons why there are times when Christians may need to move to another spiritual address.

It seems clear that God is giving you a glimpse into the real gospel and the freedom in Christ He offers—a relationship with Him, which always is more important than our relationship with a physically incorporated religious entity or set of human traditions. Trust Him, believe Him, enter into and accept His rest!

A stepdaughter living in sin

Q *I have an eighteen-year-old stepdaughter who is living in sin. She feels that not going to church makes her a bad person. Somehow she doesn't feel that gorging on food and vomiting are wrong. She doesn't feel that wearing provocative clothes or sleeping with boys is wrong. She doesn't feel that going to drug/alcohol parties is wrong.*

She was the president of her high school's Christian club last year, and she admitted that she ruined the club because she doesn't want to live like a Christian. That is the closest thing to remorse I have ever heard from her. I am at my wit's end. Her father and mother have always allowed her to do whatever she wanted. They have always told her they were proud of her. I told her that I was ashamed of her. Our fellowship has been broken.

I was a wild kid when I was her age. But at the age of twenty-two, I started going to church—although it was legalistic. After about eight years, we found a church that said it was "grace-based," but it actually believed "anything goes." It was such a relief to know that we were free from all the legalistic stuff that we didn't notice the warped doctrine to which we were being exposed.

After a few years, my husband was ordained in that church, but I was not happy with the weird stuff to which my children were being exposed.

Since I've had a religious life of being at both extremes, I really don't know how to treat my stepdaughter. I don't want to accept her immoral behavior, but I don't want to push her away from the Lord either. I'm praying about it, but would appreciate your input.

A It would seem that you have a few things to consider:
1. You are a stepmother, and your stepdaughter is not four, six, or eight years old—she is eighteen! How much help can you be, or how much influence can you be expected to supply? Perhaps you shouldn't expect too much from your contributions.

2. On top of all of this, you report that you have already had a falling-out. So you are at another disadvantage because of this.

3. Your stepdaughter seems to think that attending church will somehow make everything okay. She needs to understand that there is more to a relationship with God than going through the right religious motions.

I believe I understand what you mean about having an experience with two extremes. However, you must understand that God's grace and legalistic religion are not two equally inadequate spiritual extremes. Grace is the answer for legalism. There are places and times when grace is abused, when it is misunderstood, and when it becomes an excuse for "do-as-you-please-ism"—but abuses of God's grace do not define or nullify it. Misunderstanding God's grace does not mean that God and His grace is permissive. God's grace is anything but. Legalism, on the other hand, is a virus that can erode and destroy hope, joy, and the new life of Christ.

Authoritarianism—the real problem?

Q *I believe that legalism does not infect church congregations generally, but almost exclusively works its insidious corruption through the authorities and governing bodies of churches. I believe that legalism is a product of authoritarianism. I believe authoritarianism is the real problem.*

Jesus Christ alone is in authority over His body, the church. Jesus Christ alone is able to lead each member of His body through the Spirit without the need for authoritative human intervention. Authoritarianism is the real problem. What do you think?

A Thank you for your comments. I agree with you on some points; I differ with you on others:

1. Legalism infects every human being. We default to legalism. We resist grace, and, like iron filings to a magnet or moths to a light bulb, are fatally attracted to religious pills, potions, panaceas, and prescriptions. Legalism is a virus. It is a particular weakness for anyone who has been weakened by its relentless attacks—like an alcoholic or a malaria survivor. Legalism leaves spiritual scar tissue.

2. Authoritarianism accentuates legalism. Legalism is already present. Authoritarianism exploits it, like a drug dealer who sells to junkies.

3. I agree with you that Jesus alone is Lord and Savior. He alone saves us; He alone has the right to tell us what to do, when to do it, and how to do it. Ironically, He doesn't engage in nearly as much of that kind of thing as some of His self-appointed representatives do.

4. The body of Christ consists of all those who believe in Him as Lord and Savior—the universal church. It is not a

single organization, but the believers who make up the body of Christ are also part of many organizations, churches, fellowships, and ministries. These groups and organizations exist to help believers collectively accomplish the will of Christ.

5. Christians, therefore, are not islands of anarchy. We are all accountable. Children have parents, adults have teachers and supervisors, and we all have police and judges to whom we must answer. Romans 13 discusses the whole issue of civil authority, even when that authority does not wield the law/rules in the most appropriate way. So, while we are free in Christ, that freedom is not only freedom *from* but also freedom *to*. We are free *from* the impositions and baggage of legalism, but our freedom is not given so that we can each subjectively determine what is right and wrong. Our lives are not our own. We are bought and paid for; our mission is to serve the Lord. We are free *to* serve Him, to act in concert with the body of which He is the head. That means being cooperative, accepting a less-glorious role than others—perhaps a subordinate role, playing "second fiddle."

The bottom line is that both society and Christianity need authority to function; otherwise we would have anarchy. There is a place for human authority in the body of Christ, but there should not be a place for authoritarianism.

BIBLE

Has the New Testament been paganized?

Q *I have a nagging doubt about the authenticity of the New Testament records—whether they survived the first few hundred years intact and whether they were corrupted with other religions.*

A common argument employed by those who would discredit Christianity is to allege that the Jesus stories are influenced heavily by various pagan sun-god myths from numerous cultures. Many trace certain events in Jesus' recorded life, especially the virgin birth, healings, walking on water, Resurrection, and Ascension in a cloud, back through pagan "mystery" religions and ultimately back to Egyptian times, particularly the "savior god" Osiris. According to some accounts, this god died for his people so that his followers could inherit eternal afterlife. Some ancient art depicts Osiris in a crucifixion position. His followers, believing his body was present in the earth, ate wheat bread to inherit his promise, a kind of primitive Eucharist. Jesus coming in clouds, bringing light to the darkness, and walking on water (an ancient belief that the reflection on a lake was the sun walking on water) are alleged to be other sun-god myths.

To a human mind, especially a modern one, believing a religion based on a god-man who was virgin-born and resurrected takes a lot of faith. We simply don't experience anything like that in our lives. I have always believed the New Testament accounts of Jesus. But if the New Testament itself was paganized, where does that leave us?

A The existence in pagan cultures of Christianlike epics and themes is not a proof against the unique claims of Christianity. Christianity has never based its authority on the complete uniqueness of practices and traditions. The Bible does not claim that all Christian traditions and teachings are absolutely original. In terms of Christian faith and practice, sole claim for authenticity does not belong to the first documented record about a practice or belief. The Bible does not claim that all elements and traditions in either Old Covenant or New Covenant are unique, never heard of in any other culture. Solomon opined that there is nothing new under the sun.

The unique claims of Christianity do involve God, in the Person of Jesus, coming to this earth to suffer for and along with His creation. No other religion makes any such claim.

As for the authenticity of New Testament records, no other book claiming to be the revelation of God has survived such a critique as the Bible. More books have been written trying to undo the Bible than all other "holy" books combined. No other "holy" book can claim the antiquity, the accuracy, the authenticity with historical records, the prophetic claims that occurred, and the support of the relatively new science of archaeology.

Don't worry about struggling with these and similar questions. Your questions are natural, and beyond that, a sign of spiritual health. Too many people gullibly and religiously accept anything a religious authority says. It is reasonable and wise for us to research what happened two thousand or more years ago, even in the context of faith.

Can a two-thousand-year-old book apply to a twenty-first-century Indian?

Q *I am a third-year medical student writing from India. I have heard it said that the truth of the Bible is absolute—true for all people at all times at all places regardless of culture, ethnicity, or nationality.*

But the Gospels and the Epistles were written to a specific group of people in a specific context addressing specific situations. How does that apply to me, an Indian, separated by two thousand years from biblical events, by thousands of miles from biblical geography, and most of all by a vast cultural separation from those people to whom it was written?

A According to the Bible, God has revealed His plan to us through general revelation—the creation itself— and through special revelation—the Bible. The Bible is not a book that was written in heaven and then parachuted down to earth via an angelic flyover. God could have, of course, given us the Bible in such a way, but He did not. He determined to use humans in the authorship, translation, preservation, printing, and promulgation of the Bible.

The Bible itself is a record of God's dealings with humanity. God's methodology in giving us the Bible required God speaking to and inspiring specific people at specific times. That does not mean that the teaching or relevance of the specific event was completely limited to the original audience and recipients, for if that were the case, why have a Bible? They didn't need a Bible; they'd already received the message.

It is true that the Old Testament is specifically about one people group, one national entity—the Hebrews, the nation of

Israel, or as they are also called, the Jews. But this exclusive relationship ended with the coming of Jesus Christ. When Jesus came as God in the flesh, He came in time, in history (to the land we know as Palestine and/or Israel) with a gender (male) and race (Jewish). He came to a culture in which the Jews still regarded themselves as the exclusive people of God and all others as Gentiles. But Jesus came to this earth inclusively, not exclusively. Perhaps no passage in the New Testament better expresses Jesus' mission in this regard than Ephesians 2:11–22.

If the Bible does not apply to you—an Indian living two thousand years from the time of Jesus' birth, life, death, and resurrection—then it does not apply to me, as a German-American living during this same time, or to the Chinese, the French, the Nigerians, etc. And, for that matter, if what you imply is true, the Bible has not been relevant to anyone other than the original recipients, anyone who lived at any time, for the past two thousand years.

But the claims of the Bible, particularly of the New Covenant given to all humanity because of the sacrificial love of Jesus Christ, are for all of us, whenever we might live, whatever our background, race, creed, gender, or color. God gave us His Son because He loved the world (John 3:16), not because He loved one racial group more than others.

Is there any significance to numbers used in the Bible?

Q *In my former church, I was taught a lot about the significance of certain numbers—seven, twelve, and so on—and their importance in the unfolding of God's ongoing work with* *man. Is there really any essential God-purposed meaning to the occurrence and recurrence of particular numbers in the Bible?*

A I believe that there are times when specific numbers used in the Bible have special significance, and that obviously those numbers are used by God's inspiration. Several factors to keep in mind to maintain a balanced perspective:

1. Not all numbers used in the Bible have a special significance. The context of the passage under question can help us determine any special meaning.

2. Numbers like six, seven, twelve, and forty that often have significance in one context in which they are used do not always have that same significance in every part of the Bible. The context usually determines any added meaning.

3. Events and teachings in the Bible do not generally depend upon the use of a number which may have significance. The number, if it has any significance, may add an additional layer of meaning but never gives primary meaning. Put another way, the message of the Bible, and of the gospel in particular, can be understood perfectly without resorting to the interpretation and meaning of numbers.

4. Therefore, at the very best, the whole study of the significance of numbers in the Bible is an extra, a "fringe benefit." At the worst, numerology can take us into esoteric and bizarre beliefs far from the gospel of Jesus Christ. Any study of the significance of numbers must be approached in a balanced manner; such a study must always be seen as a minor emphasis and never assume primary significance.

It is easy to obsess over numerology and in the process miss the meaning of any passage, and especially the gospel of Jesus Christ.

STAYING AWAY FROM "THE WORLD"

Should Christians avoid non-Christians?

Q *I attended a Bible study recently where the pastor taught that Christians should not be friends with non-Christians. His biblical basis was 2 Corinthians 6:14–18. If this scripture really says that, then I am really distraught as I have many friends who are non-Christians. What is your belief on this matter? Should I not have non-Christian friends? If so, where does the Bible teach that?*

A The interpretation given to this verse by the pastor you heard is wrong. This passage is at best a principle about intermingling the sacred with the secular, and perhaps a caution against being "yoked" in some kind of contractual, binding relationship. That is, a believer should beware of ongoing intimate business relationships with those who do not share Christian values and beliefs. A similar application might be made to marriages.

This passage in 2 Corinthians can be extended to ridiculous lengths and unfortunately is (i.e., we should not buy fast food from a non-Christian, we should not buy a car or house from a non-Christian or through non-Christian salespeople, or indeed, as you report, we should not have any non-Christian friends). These kinds of inferences are ludicrous, for they run counter to the message of the gospel. The Bible urges Christians to be salt and light, taking the gospel of Jesus Christ to the world and sharing our faith. How can we do this if we are hunkered down in holy huddles, insulated from all the "bad people" who are not like us? The idea that Christians must keep themselves safe from "the world" is silly and completely un-Christlike. If Jesus had taken such an approach, there would be no Christianity, no cross, and no empty tomb.

Shunning sinners

Q The Bible says not to eat or associate with the sexually immoral or greedy (1 Corinthians 5:1–13). Paul also urged Titus to expel a divisive person (Titus 3:10). Yet some churches today have been sued after a pastor publicly announced that someone had sinned. Is "shunning" legalistic? It seems to be what the Bible teaches.

A Shunning, avoiding, and not eating with the immoral or greedy are specific biblical commands within specific contexts. But let's examine the implications of this practice, taken to its logical extremes. Let's assume the context concerns eating and those with whom Christians may share a meal. We will all die of hunger if we stop eating with those who are immoral or greedy. The first step will be to avoid eating with sinners in all public places: restaurants, fast-food outlets, airports, etc. The next step will be to take our meals alone, at home, but not with the immoral and greedy members of our family. The final step in starvation will be, of course, to quit feeding the immoral, greedy, sinful person we ourselves are.

The passages you quote teach us that there are times to let friends, loved ones, or family know that we do not condone an action, and that may mean temporarily suspending normal communication. The step is meant to convey disagreement with obvious and blatant sin, but not to convey a lack of love: for indeed Jesus Himself ate and drank with tax collectors and prostitutes. "Shunning" others often becomes prideful posturing, self-righteous condemnation that accomplishes very little apart from self-serving elevation of religious egos.

Can household items bring a curse?

Q *Recently, I heard a sermon about items in our homes that can bring curses. I realized I had many of these items, including a collection of CDs from the 1970s (mostly light rock and pop music); non-Christian novels which may have swear words in them; and a collection of secular women's magazines. I think you get the picture. The pastor gave an illustration of someone who had a small Buddha statue they received as a gift from friends who returned from a trip to Asia. After the statue was brought into the house, one of the children broke his leg, another one got sick, and so forth. Someone told them that it was the presence of the statue. They then proceeded to get rid of it, and after they did everything was okay again. Is this legalism? To me it seems to be so. In fact, it's almost like superstition or "hocus-pocus." I'd like your opinion, please.*

A When you say that you have heard "a sermon about items in our home that can bring curses," that phrase itself is worthy of examination. According to the sermon, "the items" which are said to possibly "bring curses" are rock 'n' roll music, non-Christian novels, and secular women's magazines—wow! I happen to know many Christians who have all three of these items in their homes, and that would include me. I listen to rock 'n' roll music (among other kinds of music), I read non-Christian novels and other literature that include swear words, and while I do not read secular women's magazines, my wife does.

I can sincerely tell you, as a child of God, a person who by God's grace lives the new life which Christ alone gives, that I am not under any such curse that this "teaching" claims. Those who yield themselves to Christ, and I presume that includes you, are not under this curse. No power or principality that would resist Christ has any power over us (Ephesians 6:10–18; 1 John 4:4), nor can it or some item curse us if we resist satanic powers (1 Peter 5:8–9; James 4:7) and if we live in Christ (and He in us).

As for the story about the idol of Buddha and the series of accidents and diseases that are alleged to have happened as long it was in the house, this is yet another proof to me that this sermon had neither biblical foundation nor did it have a basis in logic. This story about the idol of Buddha is an assertion; it has not been proven nor documented, but is simply a claim that someone has made. Even if it were documented, in order for it to be true and reasonable for others, it would need to be tested. Hundreds of families would need to have Buddha statues in their homes, and then results would need to be carefully monitored in order to determine whether a "curse" comes because of the presence of a Buddha statue. In the case of rock 'n' roll music, secular women's magazines, and non-Christian novels, I know of many homes and families where these items are present, and I am certain that their presence has not cursed the residents with broken legs, mysterious accidents, or exotic diseases.

We need to resist silly superstitions and religious hocus-pocus that can rob us of our freedom in Christ (see Galatians 5:1; 2 Corinthians 11:1–4). The "teaching" you describe to me is not Christ-centered; it is unbalanced, and it is legalistic, controlling, and manipulative. It is confusing and it is unbiblical. I pray that you will stop allowing this kind of irrational talk to be a part of your life, for it may well take you far from God's grace and the glorious gospel of Jesus Christ.

MENTAL ILLNESS

Are the mentally ill demon-possessed?

Q *Are mentally ill people actually demon-possessed? What about people who were once Christian who seem to slide into abnormal behavior? My mother was deemed paranoid-schizophrenic. Growing up with her was troubling, to say the least. People said that when she was younger, she was on fire for God; then they say pride set in. Is that all mental illness is, perhaps?*

A There is no doubt that the Bible speaks of a fallen spirit world—that Satan and his demons are real. The Bible is also clear that Christians need not fear this fallen spiritual world because, as 1 John 4:4 says, He that is within us is greater than he who is in the world.

There are some today that attribute virtually all mental and emotional dysfunctions to Satan and his demons. The Bible was written long before the age of modern psychiatry and psychology and, for that matter, nutrition and other studies. We know that there are many ways to treat those with mental illness and that many treatments have been successful. So it is an error to simply label all those who suffer from mental illness of any kind as having a "demon problem." There are chemical imbalances and a variety of factors that can be treated, and there is no reason to assume that all or even most abnormalities are the direct work of Satan.

But again, this is a complex subject, and most pastors I know who have received appropriate training and have many years of experience will know that they are not mental-health professionals. Pastors certainly can help, given biblical knowledge and a Christ-centered worldview, but I believe that pastors who base their ministry in God's grace also know their own limitations and therefore refer many of the more complex issues to those who have the training and competencies to treat them.

REINCARNATION

Is reincarnation really such a wacky idea?

Q *I'm a Christian, but the idea of reincarnation doesn't sound as wacky to me as my pastor seems to think it is. What do you think?*

A *Reincarnation* literally means "to come again, in the flesh." This belief is not to be confused with the Christian belief of Christ's *incarnation* (see Matthew 1:23; John 1:14; and 1 John 4:1–2). Reincarnation teaches that after death the soul attaches itself to another body and returns to live another life. The most common kind of reincarnation teaching comes from Hinduism and Buddhism and is based on the laws of *karma*. Karma says that what one sows in this life will be reaped in the next. Every action in this life has a consequence, according to karma.

The Bible says the essence of what karma teaches is simply a reiteration of the laws that God has set in motion—for this life. We pay consequences in our physical lives and bodies for actions that we take during our physical lives. However, there is a big difference between Christianity and beliefs about reincarnation when we come to the afterlife. The Bible is clear—the kingdom of heaven is not gained on the basis of what we do, on the merits we gain, or the works we amass (Ephesians 2:8–10). Salvation is a gift given to us by and because of the riches of God's grace, and it will not be enjoyed in someone else's body, but in our own glorified, immortal body (see 1 Corinthians 15).

The Bible teaches that the spirit and soul of humans are disembodied after death, awaiting resurrection. Reincarnation teaches that the soul becomes embodied in another body. Reincarnation is a process of perfection (performance-based religion) while the Christian belief based upon biblical teaching of the Resurrection is that resurrection is a perfected state, given and imparted by God's grace. Reincarnation is taught as an intermediate state, but resurrection is an ultimate, eternal state. Resurrection happens once to the same body; reincarnation claims to happen many times into different bodies.

Reincarnation is works-based, performance-based religion, and its appeal is widespread. One in four Americans believe in reincarnation, one in three college-aged people, and among Christians the ratio is one in five! Perhaps one of the reasons for such widespread acceptance of reincarnation within Christendom is the failure to proclaim God's grace, that He loves us without reservation, unconditionally.

TITHING AND GIVING

Is tithing a requirement for Christians?

Q *My pastor holds a different view than I do on tithing. He teaches that the Bible says in Malachi 3:8–12 that if we don't tithe (which he stresses is a full 10 percent) we are robbing God. He says if we do not tithe at least 10 percent, we are under a curse and not able to experience the full blessings that God wants to give us. I know from my study of the Scriptures that this teaching is false, for the following reasons:*

1. *This passage in Malachi was directed to the nation of Israel, which at the time was under the Old Covenant.*
2. *If Christians are to tithe the way Israel was instructed, they would need to keep the entire Old Covenant or none of it at all.*
3. *Nowhere does the New Testament mention that we are required to tithe. Instead, it talks about giving from the heart.*
4. *No follower of Christ is under a curse, because Christ became a curse for us when He was crucified—taking our punishment upon Himself.*
5. *As followers of Christ, we are not missing out on any blessings. Through Christ, we have all the blessings we could ever have.*

Should I write my pastor a letter explaining this? Should I talk to him face-to-face? Should I leave my church because of his unbiblical teachings? I have prayed that God would guide my pastor to teach sound doctrine on this issue, but maybe God expects me to do something about it. I am really confused about what I should do. I would value any advice you might have for me.

A In my opinion, you have done a superb job in laying out a summary of the Christian case against mandatory 10 percent tithing. Not only is the idea of Christians being under a curse if they do not subscribe to a part of the Old Covenant law ignoring the fact that Jesus became a curse for us (Galatians 3:13), but what your pastor is saying is the very opposite of Galatians 3:10: "All who rely on observing the law are under a curse."

The idea that unless we do or don't do something, we will "miss out" on blessings from God is religious legalism, far removed from the freedom in Christ given to us by God's grace. There are pastors and churches within Christianity that use the word *tithe* as your pastor does, but they are exceeding their authority, whatever their motive may be, in attempting to impose part of the Old Covenant upon the people of God. There are other pastors who use the word *tithe* in a different way than your pastor does; they use it non-specifically and generically to refer to giving without the imposition of a delineated amount or percentage.

But, enough commentary on the subject, which you have analyzed biblically and logically. Some practical points, some of which you raise:

First, on behalf of pastors everywhere: Pastors are always on the front line of fund-raising, budget balancing, and bill paying for a congregation. It is their job to promote steward-ship and responsible, Christ-centered giving. Sometimes pastors allow these pressures to motivate them with less-than-biblical calls for giving. So, in defense of your pastor, he may simply be attempting to keep the lights on, the air-conditioning running in the summer, and the heater working in the winter. This does not mean the end justifies the means. His message, as you describe it, is not biblically justified.

In fact, pastors actually have an opportunity and a duty to present a more-exacting level of giving, as outlined in the New Testament. The New Covenant in Jesus' blood does not limit our giving to dogmatic, ironclad percentages. It may be that some Christians should exceed the Old Covenant requirement of 10 percent because they can. Others are able to give only small amounts because of other priorities. Jesus gives us the freedom and responsibility to choose what amount is appropri-ate for us. Furthermore, giving under the New Covenant involves all of us, presenting our bodies as a living sacrifice, giving of our time and talents as well as treasures.

Yes, you should discuss this with your pastor. Whether you do so by letter or in person is a judgment call. My guess is that if you begin to communicate your misgivings by letter, you will eventually wind up discussing the topic in person. We are part of the priesthood of all believers, and thus have a responsibility to question unbiblical teaching that departs from authentic Christianity. So I believe you have a God-given responsibility to broach this matter, and I am sure you will do so respectfully.

As for leaving your church because of such an issue, there is no reason not to consider taking this step. As Christians we are part of the body of Christ, and we are led by Jesus Christ. Christians are not obligated to remain in a place where substandard or, even worse, outright error is being taught. Sometimes Christians do stay in their church in spite of a less-than-wholesome spiritual environment, trying to work within for change, and there is nothing wrong with such a practice. However, Christians must also consider their own spiritual health as they exist within a spiritually dysfunctional environment.

Didn't Jesus require tithing?

Q *If there is no New Testament basis for tithing, please explain Luke 11:42: "Woe to you Pharisees, because you give God a tenth of your mint, rue, and all other kinds of garden herbs, but you neglect justice and the love of God. You should have practiced the latter without leaving the former undone."*

The latter part of Jesus' statement indicates that Jesus did not want the Pharisees to neglect their tithes; however, He was more concerned with the Pharisees advancing justice and demonstrating their love for God. Isn't this teaching a New Testament basis for tithing?

A The Old Covenant not only mandates an exact 10 percent be paid "on the increase," but it also mandates two other tithes: one for observing Hebrew holy days and another for the welfare of widows, orphans, and the needy.

If tithing as mandated in the Old Covenant is in effect and required for Christians, then all three of these tithes (see Deuteronomy 14) are obligatory. We cannot pick and choose.

The passage about which you ask does not mandate tithing for Christians. First, the context of this statement by Jesus: in Luke 11, this section is called the six woes. These are similar to the longer account in Matthew 23—a stinging indictment by

Jesus of the legalism and judgmentalism that the Old Covenant gave rise to and, of course, by contrast, the new commandments He gave. Thus, this passage cannot be understood as normative or necessary for Christians. Second, whom was He specifically addressing? The Jews and the Pharisees. Of course they should tithe; they were Jews under the Old Covenant. The New Covenant had not yet come. The temple and temple practices still stood, not to be destroyed until A.D. 69–70 (the ramifications of that date and its meaning even for Jewish Christians are carefully addressed in the book of Hebrews).

Will God bless us in return for giving?

Q *Is it correct by God's standards to sow a seed of money and expect a harvest—either of money or something that may not be financial, such as sowing a money seed in order to get a husband or to receive good health or to get out of debt? Please help me understand Galatians 6:7.*

A It is not biblically correct to "sow a seed" of money and expect to receive a direct blessing from God, whether material or immaterial, on a one-to-one correspondence based upon the "seed that is sown." This idea is often used by churches, ministries, and pastors to motivate people to give to the work of the church. While the cause in many cases is for the gospel of the kingdom, the idea behind the promotion and motivation is biblically flawed.

The passage in Galatians 6:7 is taken out of its context and twisted into something that God, as He inspired the apostle Paul, did not intend.

One of the basic rules of understanding the Bible is to

understand the passage in its context. We need to remember that the passage had a meaning to its original audience, and we should ensure we understand that meaning first before we attempt to apply the passage to our lives.

First—the context of the book of Galatians. This book is specifically devoted to teaching against legalism, the belief that if we do certain things, then God is obligated to respond in a certain way. Paul teaches that freedom in Christ means that we are released from the basic principles of the world, which is the idea that God is so impressed with our good deeds that He will give us salvation as a result. Legalism is performance-based religion, whereas authentic Christianity is based solely on the finished work of Christ on the cross. The gospel of Jesus Christ tells us we are saved by God's grace, not by what we do. Christ did for us what we can never do for ourselves.

With that brief summary, which does not do justice to this critically important book of Galatians, we come to chapter six. Paul begins by talking about bearing each other's sins. In the verse immediately prior to the verse about which you ask, Paul tells us to "share all good things" with our spiritual instructors; and then he says, in verse seven, "Do not be deceived: God cannot be mocked. A man reaps what he sows."

Paul is addressing a practical matter, but one that has spiritual implications. At the beginning of the chapter, we are told to take care of one another and to help those who have burdens. Then he says that we should also take care of those who give us spiritual instruction, and that we will reap what we sow. It is in the context of caring for others' needs that we are told that we will reap what we sow. This passage does not include the manipulative idea that sowing a financial seed is like a spiritual investment in the heavenly stock market. Paul is *not* saying that God will make sure that our "investment" will pay dividends for us, return even more money back to us, or guarantee us better health or happier marriages.

This passage is teaching that our giving and sharing and our financial support for those who give us and others spiritual instruction is an investment, both now and for eternity. When we give of those resources with which God has blessed us, we are laying up treasures in heaven (Matthew 6:20). We are making deposits into God's kingdom of heaven and to His work being done on this earth, where help and healing is available to those who are spiritually sick, in spiritual bondage and prison. We invest into God's kingdom and to His work so that new life, the new life in Christ, can be given to those who are weak, lost, and broken.

It is in that context we will reap what we sow. That is, we will reap what we sow, and by giving of our financial resources we will help others who desperately need it. It is an erroneous conclusion to believe that reaping what we sow somehow means that we will financially benefit from our giving. Our motive in giving should be to help others, to bear the burdens of others, not some spiritual investment scheme that we believe will eventually reward us with physical benefits.

END TIMES

What is the meaning of 666?

Q *Where did the number 666 come from? How was it calculated? What is its significance?*

A In the book of Revelation, the number 666 stands for the mark of the Beast (Revelation 13:18). In order to understand any number or color or other symbol used in Revelation, one must first understand that Revelation is written in an apocalyptic style, a style that relies heavily on symbolism. Attempts to assign literal meaning and specific individuals and geo-political settings to many of the symbols in Revelation have failed—again and again, primarily because those trying to understand the book have failed to understand the style in which it is written.

According to Revelation 13, the number 666 is the number of the Beast's name. Throughout the Bible, the number six is often used to describe imperfection, often that of humans, compared to the perfection of God. In Revelation 13:18, three sixes are used together, which would seem to indicate multiplied human imperfection, the solutions and answers to human problems that man devises, the end product of human solutions and government.

Many have attempted and failed to identify this number with a specific human. If any human might be considered for this "honor," then the Roman emperor Nero would come the closest, for he epitomized evil at the time of the writing, but even that identification is not the primary message given to us by the timeless book of Revelation. Spurred on by the prospect of coming up with the specific identity of 666, many try to use elaborate codes applied to a variety of languages. If we are willing to go to elaborate lengths (and some are), it is possible to conclude that almost any human name, in some language, given some code, equals 666. That is not the teaching of Revelation 13.

Will everyone see Jesus when He returns?

Q *When Jesus returns, will everyone be able to see Him, or will only Christians? Also, what is the purpose of the Antichrist? After the Rapture, is it too late for those left behind to be saved? If the Antichrist is chained in the lake of fire for one thousand years, where will the lake of fire be and will everyone be able to see it?*

A My answer to your questions is "I don't know." Further, I don't believe anyone else does either, but that doesn't mean there aren't people who would give you some rather dogmatic responses to your queries.

Some who believe in the Rapture also believe in a loud and audible Rapture—so that everyone will see and hear Jesus return, and see and hear those who are raptured taken away. This perspective has the Rapture being a grim warning of the pain and suffering they, the "left behind," will suffer in the

Great Tribulation. Others believe in a silent Rapture, with friends and family becoming aware that loved ones are gone because they disappear, leaving clothing and personal effects where they were when the Rapture happened.

I don't believe either scenario. I don't think anyone knows such details, for the Bible doesn't furnish enough beyond-a-doubt explanations. So speculating about and predicting such things serves little purpose other than to make people afraid (not a tactic Jesus employed, by the way).

The book of Revelation says the Antichrist's purpose is, and has always been throughout almost two thousand years of Christian history, to oppose the one, true God. The book of Revelation does not specify whether the one thousand years is an exact length of time, as we humans measure time, or simply a hyperbolic term meaning "a very long time, longer than any human can imagine in his or her lifetime."

What will happen to Christians during the tribulation?

Q *Where will Christians be during the coming tribulation? Can you please explain the pre-tribulation, mid-tribulation, and post-tribulation ideas?*

A Christians are divided between a-millennial, post-millennial, and pre-millennial (that is, how to interpret passages that speak of a millennial rule of Christ and the saints).

Pre-millennial: Those who believe that the biblical events spoken of surrounding the second coming of Jesus are yet in the future.

Post-millennial: These Christians believe that a one-thousand-year millennium which follows the tribulation represents the spiritual victory of the gospel, and that Jesus will return after the spiritual victory is won by the church and the saints (as empowered by Jesus Christ). They believe that the spiritual reign of Jesus through His church prepares the way for His bodily return.

A-millennial: The belief that the one thousand years spoken of in the book of Revelation is symbolic rather than literal. Those who favor this view see the one thousand years as a long time, a non-specific period of time between the crucifixion and resurrection and the Second Coming.

Pre-, post-, and mid-tribulation ideas fall only within the pre-millennial view. These ideas are even more speculative (that is, there is little biblical evidence to be dogmatic, not that it is wrong to hold a specific view). The perspectives have a great deal to do with how believers are supposedly protected from physical suffering. Some use the word "Rapture" to convey this teaching (which is a rather modern teaching, not having been popularly taught until a little over 150 years ago). All of these posit that Christ will return at the end of a tribulation—most believe it to be seven years in length. The pre-tribulation people believe protection from the plagues and troubles of the tribulation will be given before the tribulation starts; the mid-trib folks believe physical protection is given sometime during the tribulation (so believers have to endure some of the tribulation); and others (post-trib) believe that Christians will not be saved from the physical tribulation at all.

Biblical evidence is not sufficient for any dogmatic conclusion, although there are some who believe that their way is the only way ("my way or the highway"). While some views seem more extreme and biblically illogical, I do not believe that Christians should separate and divide over such speculative teaching. We will find out after Jesus returns, and I suspect that all of our dogmatism will not mean much then.

What about the Rapture?

Q *My question is about the Rapture. I was saved and baptized in the Free Methodist church. I now attend a community church. I watched several prophecy preachers when I was first saved. They helped me a lot, but now I have doubts about the Rapture. What is your opinion about the Rapture? My grandchildren are asking me about this, and I want to speak the truth. Is there going to be a Rapture of the church before the tribulation, after the tribulation, or none at all? Also, if the Rapture is to be after or during the tribulation or not at all, why did Christ die?*

I know we could never be good enough for heaven and without Jesus' sacrifice we could never reach heaven. He died for us, for our sins. Do you see why I am having a hard time explaining to my grandchildren?

A You seem to be thinking clearly about this topic. There are biblically based questions about the Rapture teaching:

1. Christians somehow "got by" without believing in a Rapture until about 150 years ago. Why? Why didn't Christians believe in a Rapture before if it is biblical?

2. Just how biblical is the Rapture? There is one main passage in 1 Thessalonians 4:17, and maybe one or two others depending upon how they are understood. The passage speaks of believers as being "caught up in the sky" at the Second

Coming, but no other details are given. So is this enough biblical evidence to construct elaborate, dogmatic, and specific teaching about the Rapture?

3. Why do we need to worry about being left behind (as you imply in your question)? All of our worries about being left behind were answered at the cross and the empty tomb. We are not left behind, and we never will be. Jesus will never forsake us.

4. Speaking of being "left behind"—the fact is that the vast majority of Christians today, and for that matter an even bigger majority for almost 1,800 years, do not and did not believe in the Rapture. Will Christians be left behind simply because they do not believe the Rapture and preach it? What does "being left behind" tell us about God and His nature that differs with biblical teaching about God?

5. Are we in the "last days"? Christians, pastors, and laymen alike have been teaching and believing that the end will come in their generation—just a few short years, or a decade or two away is the usual message. That message has been proclaimed for more than 150 years since a man named Darby came up with a unique way to interpret the Bible called dispensationalism. What has been the fruit of all this "last days madness," this end-times "prediction addiction"? When specific predictions have failed (and all of them have so far), many have lost faith. A number have left Christianity altogether. What is the result of continuously being in some high-pitched, feverish state of anxiety, thinking the end is only a few years away?

6. The Rapture teaching causes Christians to be concerned about saving their own necks and those of their loved ones. The efforts that they take to ensure that they will be raptured are far closer to religious legalism than they are to the glorious gospel of the grace of Jesus Christ. All of this end-times mad-

ness is just that; it is causing Christians to be mocked by the world at large. It is misrepresenting God. It is causing many to lose faith when prophecies fail, and it is causing many to turn inward, worried about saving themselves.

AND IN CONCLUSION —THE ULTIMATE ANSWER

Don't you just hate it when you are in church, and the preacher finally utters those sweet words of promise— "and in conclusion" —but your idea of a conclusion and his are like ships passing in the night? When you hear the words "and in conclusion," you heave a sigh of relief and start dreaming about beating the lunch crowd at your favorite restaurant, but the preacher keeps going on and on and on. Okay, I'll make this brief (that's another thing that preachers like me say that drives me crazy because when they do I know it will be anything but brief).

In the Introduction, I invited you, in case you didn't like my answers, to improvise your own Christ-centered solutions. Let me reinforce that invitation. Life is, in many ways, an endless series of questions and dilemmas. In the twenty-first century, the questions have become more complex, perhaps because we are living on top of so many cultures that have gone before us. Their contributions, as well as their unanswered questions, are part of our legacy.

In reality, every generation since Adam and Eve has searched for answers. In the church world, we have decided to call people who are looking for answers "seekers"—and while that's a great description, let's not fool ourselves by thinking that spiritual seekers first arrived during our generation! Let's also realize that we are all seekers, for the questions of our lives will never be fully answered while we are in this body of flesh. We are all seeking, we are all searching, and we are all on a spiritual journey. In some ways we are spiritual explorers, and our adventure is never over, not until we leave this earth and journey to eternity, to the place that Jesus has prepared for us.

As you continue your own journey for truth, always base your quest in Christ—look to Him as the ultimate Answer for all your questions. It is easy to become side-tracked by basing your quest for truth and meaning on yourself and your own limitations. You can easily see yourself as your own fixer—and there are religious voices that will encourage you to see your efforts as of first importance in finding the ultimate answer.

However, when we assume sole responsibility for solving our questions and dilemmas, our lives become one big self-improvement project. Off we go on an unending cycle of places to go and things to do—all in the name of finding truth, fulfillment, meaning, and significance. When our efforts are the foundation of our search for answers, we become our own project—so in search of answers we earn a degree, get that promotion, work on a relationship, try to become a better parent, exercise, diet, take our vitamins, read more books, and go to church more (because the more we go to church, the more answers we will have, right?) and, of course, we try to stop doing the bad stuff we know we shouldn't.

There's nothing wrong with doing and not doing all that stuff, but all that stuff is not where you will find the ultimate Answer. Jeremiah was one of the great prophets of Israel. Jeremiah lived the life of those to whom he ministered—his life was an ongoing roller-coaster ride of hope and certainty that came out of deep conflict and despair. The book of Jeremiah leaves no doubt that Jeremiah never ran out of questions.

In chapters 30–33, the nation of Judah is about to be captured and taken captive by the Babylonians. In the besieged city of Jerusalem, overwhelmed by famine and hardship, Jeremiah finds himself faced not only with those problems but with the fact that he is held prisoner because he had recommended that people leave Jerusalem and avoid the certain bloodshed that would occur at its fall.

During this painful and difficult time, God gave Jeremiah encouragement that rings true for us today. Even while the destruction of Judah and Jerusalem, its capital city, was obviously near and inevitable, and even though Jeremiah found himself a prisoner on top of it all, God reminded Jeremiah that He was the source of any answer Jeremiah needed. "Call to me and I will answer you and tell you great and unsearchable things you do not know" (Jeremiah 33:3).

As you are faced with the dilemmas and questions of your life, by all means use all of the resources available to you. Do what you can do. But in all of your doing, make sure that you call out to God, for no matter how much you do, no matter how much you may accomplish, without God we will never find the ultimate Answer.

Rate this book! On a scale of zero to ten, where ten is "definitely" and zero means "absolutely not," would you recommend this book to a friend? Please tell us. Go to **www.thomasnelson.com/rateit** and click the number indicating your choice. It's a fast, easy, way to lend your voice to the publishing process.

Love to read? Get excerpts from new books sent to you by email. Join Shelf Life, Thomas Nelson's FREE online book club. Go to **www.thomasnelson.com/shelflife**.

MORE ABOUT
GREG ALBRECHT
AND PLAIN TRUTH
MINISTRIES

Our Mission

We lead people to Jesus Christ and the freedom of authentic Christianity with the plain, clear, and sensible teachings of the Bible. We help to change lives by introducing people to God and His amazing grace.

We focus on Jesus Christ and God's grace, offering hope, insight, and encouragement in a world of religious legalism. We provide teaching, resources, and assistance for Christians of all denominations. We serve those who are burned out with organized religion and provide spiritual nourishment for those who have been oppressed and taken advantage of in the name of God.

- PTM proclaims God's love.
- PTM advocates essential, biblically based Christian doctrines.
- PTM stands against the deadly virus of legalism.
- PTM provides help and healing for refugees from religious legalism and authoritarian churches.

- PTM communicates its message electronically and in print, in its magazines, books and booklets, audio cassettes, CDs, letters, radio, pod-casts, e-mail, and on the Internet.

- PTM is a member of the Evangelical Press Association (EPA) and National Religious Broadcasters (NRB).

Our Statement of Faith

- GOD

We believe in one eternal, triune God in three co-essential, yet distinct Persons: Father, Son, and Holy Spirit.

- JESUS CHRIST

We believe in the Lord Jesus Christ, begotten of the Holy Spirit, born of the Virgin Mary, fully God and fully human, the Son of God and Lord of all, worthy of worship, honor, and reverence, who died for our sins, was raised bodily from the dead, ascended to heaven, and will come again as King of kings.

- THE HOLY SCRIPTURES

We believe that the Bible constitutes the accurate, infallible, and divinely inspired written Word of God, the foundation of truth, the fully reliable record of God's revelation to humanity.

- SALVATION

We believe that human salvation is the gift of God, by grace through faith in Jesus Christ, not earned by personal merit or good works.

- THE CHURCH

We believe in the spiritual unity of believers in our Lord Jesus Christ.

WHAT WE DO

Christianity Without the Religion

Join Greg Albrecht, president of Plain Truth Ministries, at www.ptm.org for a new and revolutionary kind of church service. In our half-hour service, you'll find the freedom of authentic, pure, and genuine Christianity—Christianity without walls or denominational barriers—Christianity without humanly imposed rules, rituals, and regulations. In short, you'll find Christianity Without the Religion—a fresh, new approach to weekly worship. Available at www.ptm.org twenty-four hours a day, with a new service posted every Sunday morning.

Plain Truth Magazine

A refreshing voice in Christian journalism, *Plain Truth* is bold and uncompromising—it addresses topics and issues that other magazines might avoid—it challenges unbiblical and cultic practices and ideas that may have become popular within Christendom. *Plain Truth* is published bi-monthly. A free introductory one-year subscription is available for the asking in the United States and Canada.

Plain Truth Radio

Hosted by Greg Albrecht, daily *Plain Truth* radio is a half-hour program available twenty-four hours a day on our website at www.ptm.org. *Plain Truth* radio is Christian radio with a difference. Greg's heartfelt messages help listeners deal with the day-to-day issues that face them. Many programs and topics are available on audio cassette or CD—see our resource listing or website for a selection.

Books by Greg Albrecht

Bad News Religion: The Virus That Attacks God's Grace.
A guide to the most dangerous spiritual virus of the twenty-first century—the deadly virus of religious legalism—the idea that you can do something that will make God more pleased with you. *Bad News Religion* shows you how to spot legalism and tells how to identify healthy, Christ-centered, grace-based Christianity.

Revelation Revolution: The Overlooked Message of the Apocalypse is a revolution in the way that many have been trained and taught to think about biblical prophecy. *Revelation Revolution* is a grace-based, Christ-centered exploration of the biblical book of Revelation. Join many others in beginning to understand what the Bible's most misunderstood book really means.

PTM Weekly E-mail Update

Wherever you may be in this world, every week in your e-mail box you can receive an update from PTM—packed with news, perspective, commentary, and Q&As. Read feedback, pro and con, from listeners, readers, and supporters. Sign up on our website or e-mail us at ptmupdate@ptm.org.

Let Us Know How We May Serve You

PLAIN TRUTH
MINISTRIES

Mailing Address:
Plain Truth Ministries
Pasadena, CA 91129

Website:
www.ptm.org

Call Toll-Free:
1-800-309-4466